Intergenerational Practice in Schools and Settings

Intergenerational Practice in Schools and Settings provides guidance through the many approaches in education that bring generations together. Identifying the purpose of intergenerational practice, this book offers an insight into how other educational settings have used programmes to enhance the learning experience and connect students to their community and local environment.

Serving as a practical guide on setting up an intergenerational programme and identifying how to overcome the barriers that educators may face as they progress, this engaging book provides the knowledge and skills needed for developing sustainable projects and provides students with the opportunity to enhance the world around them. With case studies from a range of educators and practitioners, this book encourages readers to reflect on how to establish multi-agency relationships to create mutual learning spaces for different generations.

Intergenerational Practice in Schools and Settings is an accessible text to understand the evidence behind the approach, with experiences from educators who are fully engaged with intergenerational practice. It is an inspirational guide for experienced educators, trainee students interested in adopting an intergenerational approach, and for those with prior experience in the field, providing a rationale of how to develop and extend intergenerational opportunities.

Fey Cole is a Further and Higher Education Lecturer, and a Teaching and Learning Advisor in Northern Ireland.

Intergenerational Practice in Schools and Settings
An Educator's Handbook

Fey Cole

LONDON AND NEW YORK

Cover image: © Getty Images

First published 2023
by Routledge
4 Park Square, Milton Park, Abingdon, Oxon OX14 4RN

and by Routledge
605 Third Avenue, New York, NY 10158

Routledge is an imprint of the Taylor & Francis Group, an informa business

© 2023 Fey Cole

The right of Fey Cole to be identified as author of this work has been asserted in accordance with sections 77 and 78 of the Copyright, Designs and Patents Act 1988.

All rights reserved. No part of this book may be reprinted or reproduced or utilised in any form or by any electronic, mechanical, or other means, now known or hereafter invented, including photocopying and recording, or in any information storage or retrieval system, without permission in writing from the publishers.

Trademark notice: Product or corporate names may be trademarks or registered trademarks, and are used only for identification and explanation without intent to infringe.

British Library Cataloguing-in-Publication Data
A catalogue record for this book is available from the British Library

ISBN: 978-1-032-20212-9 (hbk)
ISBN: 978-1-032-20213-6 (pbk)
ISBN: 978-1-003-26268-8 (ebk)

DOI: 10.4324/9781003262688

Typeset in Bembo
by Newgen Publishing UK

Contents

Acknowledgements vii

Introduction 1

1 What is intergenerational practice? 4

2 Moving beyond an annual carol service 14

3 Global approaches to intergenerational practice 24

4 Building societies where all generations come together 31

5 Overcoming barriers to intergenerational practice 39

6 The benefits of intergenerational learning and practice for students 53

7 The benefits of intergenerational practice for communities 62

8 How to make intergenerational practice work in education 72

9 Adopting a multidisciplinary approach to intergenerational practice 79

10 Planning for intergenerational practice 84

11 Intergenerational practice in action 94

12	Evaluating intergenerational projects	104
13	Social action and shifting perspectives	114
	Conclusion	118
	References	121
	Index	126

Acknowledgements

This book would not have happened if it were not for the generations before me. You are now with me as I hear the birds sing, I see the sunrise and I smell the bloom of a new bud. Nanny Clark and Nana, you were exceptional women who taught me love, laughter and compassion. Nana, you always wanted your stories to continue through the generations, so I hope I have captured some of them here with honour.

My journey would not have started into Early Years if it were not for you, Clare Beer. Thank you for believing in me and for my first chapter in my vocation. We love you.

For all the people who have shared their story with me as I have researched for this book, I cannot thank you enough for your insight into intergenerational practice. It really has brought much happiness to learn from you all and I am very humbled to have been able to capture your words. To the team at Linking Generations, you are inspiring advocates who I have gained so much from, thank you for all that you do.

Particular gratitude must go to the team I work with and who started the intergenerational journey with me: Shirley-Anne McAdam, Carmel McGeary and Gillian Greenaway. I really do feel very lucky to work with such wonderful friends and inspiring educators. Thanks must also go to Linda Beatty for her kindness and laughter that is woven into every day at work, *xièxie* for always encouraging me. Susanne Workman, thank you for your wisdom and commitment to Further Education. You reminded me to focus from the heart.

To my constant role model, Fiona Johnstone-Clark. I could not have asked for a better mother. You gave me every opportunity and smashed every glass ceiling. Your heart is ever giving and I am thankful you are my closest friend. You are an exceptional person.

There are two communities of practice I must acknowledge. The #JoyFE Collective, if it were not for you I would not have been brave enough to send off my proposal for this book. I am inspired by you every day and it is truly amazing the work that is done by you all to bring soul into education. We are making change. To the #EYTagteam Community, I appreciate the kindness and openness of you all and the commitment to our children. Investment in the Early Years will move forward through to the next generation.

For my mother-in-law Elizabeth Cotterell, thank you for always being there with ease when we've needed an extra hour or a last-minute pick-up and checking in on how I really am with a cup of tea at hand. We really do appreciate you.

Of course my biggest thanks has to go to my home team – the Coles. Richard, I have no greater champion than you. We have taught the children what real love looks like and there is no greater lesson than that. To Ruby, Matilda and Henry, I do all of this for you. The three of you make me proud every day and I hope one day you read this book and you feel our family values threaded through it. Always take care of one another and find work that makes you feel good. My heart is full because of the three of you.

I am very grateful to Routledge Publishing for making this book happen. My hope is for it to spark creative thinking that makes a positive impact on our society.

And to my dear friends Vicky, Jax, Jennifer and Nicola. Thank you for being you. "We all need our friends": wise words, Mrs. H.

This book is for every educator who is led by values and commitment to doing better. In case no one else has told you recently, I believe in you. Make a change, be brave. Go forward with love and embrace every opportunity that sparks joy.

Introduction

Life has changed considerably over the last few decades. Technological advancements, rises in global population, climate change and shifts in the labour market have all been key factors in our approach to family life. Change always brings with it both positives and negatives but one area we see impacted greatly is a loss of connection between generations. In order for our communities to thrive, we all need to feel safe, secure and confident in their surroundings. There needs to be spaces for all within our society in order to come together and create shared values in environments that reflect the diverse individuals which our society comprises. From the children to the elderly members of the community, we need to recognise that we should do more to hear the voice of every individual and recognise their worth in order for them to feel the community is theirs and that it is somewhere that reflects their hopes, desires and needs.

We need societies where everybody's voice is heard and recognised. From policy makers to neighbours, the importance of connecting together has never been more vital to ensure social isolation and disengagement does not impact on those marginalised within society. Those of us working in educational settings hold the key to being able to open purposeful spaces where different generations can come together for friendship, learning and deeper connections to our local environments. As you read this book, I would encourage you to reflect on your own practice and curriculum to consider how investing in intergenerational learning will benefit all those who participate.

In many ways, our world could not be more connected than it currently is. Social media has enabled us to stay in contact with old friends and find new ones. The 2020 Covid-19 pandemic showed us how technology could allow work and social groups to continue to connect despite us all staying at home. But do these online tools really connect us? Social media is designed in a way to surround us with people with similar interests, viewpoints and lifestyles. We can find it very difficult to move out of the online echo chamber. The importance of children and young people connecting with diverse groups of individuals is essential for their sense of belonging, their understanding of the world around them and for communities to prosper. We need our children to be exposed to different viewpoints so that they are able to make sense of their own being and values, as they transition through life into adulthood. We want our children to grow into independent, secure individuals, and we are able to support this by surrounding them with different people, teaching them to move outside the echo chamber and to be authentic to themselves.

As someone who is a fan of social media for learning, using it frequently within my teaching practice and for my own development and connections, I also recognise the pitfalls. We need to create opportunities for children and young people to be able to share and listen to others. Storytelling and listening are art forms that we are losing in parts of the online world, and although there are spaces in which people are still able to do this well, this is outnumbered by the number of online spaces where people do not reflect on what they see, say, hear or read. Throughout this book you will hear the stories of the ability of those engaged in intergenerational practice to gain insight and understanding of the benefits it has brought to them as educators and to the pupils with whom they work, alongside their wider community. For many of us, when we reflect on our experiences with older members of our family, we often think about the stories that they shared with us. Personally, some of my favourite memories of childhood were sitting at my nanny and nana's knees listening to them tell me a variety of stories from their past. This gave me a link to my history, allowed me to learn about how things were in years gone by and taught me a great deal about what is important in life. Their tales were chequered with stories that made me laugh, made me smile and sometimes made me sad. I was able to explore an array of deep emotions with people with whom I felt safe and secure, a skill vitally needed for our emotional wellbeing. Many of my core values come from my time sitting alongside them and playing with their buttons and pearls – and intergenerational experiences can provide that sense of security for the children and young people that we work with, providing them with times within their routine to explore the immense spectrum of emotions we feel on a daily basis.

In a world that sees us fragmented from one another in many ways, it is through physical connections that we are able to develop the skills needed for sustainable and happy environments for growth and mindset. This book evaluates the benefits that intergenerational practice brings to education, communities and individuals. You will be encouraged to think outside the box and to be creative in your approach in order to give the children and young people you work with the opportunity to learn in a dynamic and productive way that supports these relationships and encourages young people to be curious. We will reflect on how we can break down barriers to intergenerational practice and explore how we can use online resources effectively for connections across generations. By creating intergenerational spaces, we are able to bridge the gap that has been created within society where people come together and offer a much richer and diverse learning experience to our children and young people.

The perceptions of old age are changing. With people living longer and healthier lives, the old age we remember of our grandparents may be very different to our children's. Retirement is often the time when we would consider someone to be in their older stage of life, however, within the United

Kingdom there is no defined age as to when someone is able to retire. The World Health Organization suggests between 60 and 65 years of age is when the older stage of life begins and is the typical retirement age. With many of us living into our eighties and nineties, our sixties still bring with it many years of living ahead. Where governments and policy makers define us by our economic status, many of us will define older age by how we feel and how we appear to others. As we engage in intergenerational programmes we may find ourselves, as practitioners, eventually falling into the older age bracket. I would encourage you to see past the labelling of age status and to instead reflect on the individuals and how their wealth of experience, skills and knowledge can be shared with the children and young people in a space that is equal in partnership.

Throughout each chapter, we will consider how we can break down barriers through intergenerational practice. We will review the benefits and need to work across generations and then evaluate how we are able to implement different types of intergenerational learning within our own educational establishments. It will showcase how this has been tested in a number of different types of provision and gain feedback from different participants and educational professionals who have engaged in different activities and brought their own communities together. Whether you are already involved in intergenerational practice or are just starting out on your journey, this book will offer you the opportunity to develop your ideas and reflect on how it can support the learning and emotional wellbeing of the children, young people and families that you work with. In a world where we have access to such an immense scope of information, I hope you will be encouraged to think about what is directly in front of you and how we keep local people and environments connected.

Intergenerational practice is not new. It is, however, becoming increasingly identified as an area of focus within education, social care and community planning. There have been a number of factors that have left many communities fragmented, and time together is sometimes difficult to find nowadays due to the scope of responsibilities that we find upon us. Throughout this handbook we explore how you can adopt a systematic approach to intergenerational practice and use it as a way of connecting all of the generations within communities and creating activities and spaces that value and recognise the contributions of all. We will investigate both the importance of generations learning together and how this can be implemented within your own practice and institutions. Intergenerational practice is a shared practice: it requires all of those involved to work collaboratively together and to be open to learn and appreciate the stories of others; respecting the different experiences and attributes that everyone brings. I hope that by trying out your own projects, you will find as much joy as I did from being part of a successful intergenerational learning environment. This is your starting point, embrace it and enjoy every moment that sees you more engaged and secure within your community and the wider collaborative intergenerational family that comes with these projects.

1 What is intergenerational practice?

Why intergenerational practice?

When I submitted the proposal of this book, I spent the rest of the afternoon following our usual routine. The routine is a busy one with work and family demands. As I dropped my eldest daughter off at work, I sat in the car for a few moments and checked my emails on my phone. A knock on the glass made me jump and I rolled down the window to greet an elderly gentleman who introduced himself as my eighteen-year-old daughter's friend. I have to admit, I was a little perplexed but also intrigued. He asked if I had time to talk, and I could feel my mind mentally checking in on 50 different "to do" tabs. I replied that I had time and found myself sitting on the roadside for the next 25 minutes hearing all about this man's truly wonderful life. We found commonality; he had lived in London close to where my extended family are. We discussed differences. He asked quite openly about my religious beliefs and we compared these. He reminded me of my grandmother's tales as he talked about the old dance halls he used to frequent and we talked about how the village has changed from before I had ever been around. We discussed finances and how families afford to live on small wages and how he manages his pension. Then he went on to talk about his routine, the people who surround this. My daughter, serving him in the shop and taking the time to have a conversation with him being an integral part of this. After 25 minutes, he had to leave to get his dinner served from the home help who visited, and I was left with a warmth from the connection I had made that day.

Meeting him will stay with me and it now brings a wave and a chat whenever I pass by the gentleman in the car. That knock on the window initially scared me a little, but it gave me a choice to either be present in my community or rush off to the next errand. I cannot stress enough how much I learnt from his stories that day and the joy I got from sharing them with my family later that evening. Intergenerational learning can be as informal as that at times, taking time to actively listen and to share stories together in order to learn from one another. I share this story as I have seen first-hand the value of intergenerational learning for all involved. Both of us gained something from that impromptu exchange and, when intergenerational spaces are created in settings, we find ourselves with opportunities that have not presented themselves before. Our educational systems need to be built on people, and we need our young people to see that they are part of a much wider society that loves and cares for one another. Our position of being a role model to the children we work with brings great responsibility – and what better way can we do that then by showing them that we value everyone within society and that everyone within our society has something to offer?

I hope that this book challenges you to think outside the box, to be brave in your approach and to bring something new to your pedagogy. My own experience in intergenerational learning has changed my outlook as an educator, and the path I have been on to get there has been an exciting one. Along the way I have met with a wealth of individuals who have taught me the skills and understanding of how to implement purposeful activities that bring benefit to both children and older generations.

As you embark on your commitment to intergenerational practice, I encourage you to do it with an open heart and with the focus on what can come from connections. The society we live in and the lifestyles we have are fast-paced, and this can sometimes lead us to neglect our emotional health. My experiences of intergenerational practice, and my conversations with other educational professionals who have been involved in it, has shown me the benefits it brings not only to learning opportunities but also to our wellbeing and sense of belonging. Intergenerational learning allows us to deliver the necessary curriculums we follow, whilst also showing children and young people a wealth of options available ahead of them. Intergenerational experiences in schools and colleges embrace a hopeful curriculum that encourages us to be brave, build on our communication skills and take the time to care for one another. These skills are essential for contentment and happiness as we progress in life. Your first step in implementing intergenerational practice is here, and I wish you every success in opening up your provision to a wealth of new opportunities.

What is intergenerational practice?

The Beth Johnson Foundation (2001) defines intergenerational practice as an approach that "aims to bring people together in purposeful, mutually beneficial activities which promote greater understanding and respect between generations and contribute to building more cohesive communities".

By bringing generations together we have the ability to increase the connections between people and in turn, generate a society where shared values and support mechanisms are increased. The intergenerational practice within your organisation has the scope to ripple outside of the institution, creating spaces for the sharing of knowledge and skills between the young and old. This community-focussed approach, where there is mutual respect and purposeful activities, brings with it more cohesive societies and an abundance of learning opportunities for all age groups. There are two types of intergenerational practice: learning and care, and this book will focus on the educational benefits that come from being together. As you read through each chapter and adopt your own projects within this area, you will begin to understand how closely linked the two elements of intergenerational practice are. As educators, we focus on the learning within our planning but adopt a person-centred approach throughout and this will support us in building secure and encouraging environments for all involved.

The fragmentation of society sees people from the youngest of years separated into age-based activities and learning spaces. Our children attend toddler groups, they go to sports training according to their school year. Full-time college courses tend to be for those in their later teen years and senior social sessions are held by community organisations. This fragmentation is evident in nearly everything we do, and from the moment we are born we find ourselves conformed to fit within boxes defined by our age and status. There is an increasing awareness in people of the need for generations to come together and share their learning, knowledge and social experiences in order to build and enrich our communities. This separation leads to a fear of breaking free from these constraints and many missed opportunities for our communities to come together in an enabling environment. Once we overcome this fear, we are able to see how easy it is to adopt an intergenerational approach and it leads us to wonder why we do not come together more.

The difference between intergenerational care and intergenerational learning

When planning for intergenerational practice it is vital to understand what you hope to achieve through the implementation of projects. For those in education, I would expect that your focus will be on intergenerational learning in order to incorporate the activities into pupils' educational plans. We will review each of these practices in further detail but for now it is important for us to understand that the two areas vary in their approach. Intergenerational care focusses on how we bring generations together in shared spaces and this can be purely for social purposes and connection. It could be observed through lunches with care home residents and nursery children joining together, or nurseries and care homes co-located on the same site. Intergenerational learning adopts methods of practice that provide a framework for generations to co-learn together. As educators, we need to ensure that what we are doing within our sessions is purposeful and brings learning to both the children and the adults in attendance. This emphasis on both parties learning is vital for intergenerational learning, and the activities should not be designed where the sessions only focus on the educational needs of the children and young people with whom you work.

As educators, you will find that by creating spaces where generations come together, there is often a blend of the two areas of care and learning due to it being more social than our usual classroom experiences. This can be a strength of a successful intergenerational experience. Your focus on the physical environment will need to ensure that you meet with the care needs of all those participating and that everyone can feel at ease for meaningful exchanges. There will be conversations and activities that organically present themselves and it is important to value the social and emotional connections that come during your activities. Intergenerational practice slows down our strategies in a positive way and allows us to see the potential of what comes for our children and young people from the social side of spending time together. By blending care and learning, we are able to focus on the individual needs of those that we are working with.

A key framework for Western education follows the influence of theorists such as Abraham Maslow's and his hierarchy of needs (1943). As educators, we are aware of the importance of considering the underpinning needs of individuals, in order for them to excel to their full potential. Maslow's work was heavily influenced by his anthropological research study with the Blackfoot community in the River Valley of Saskatchewan, Canada, and their wisdom and culture provides us with an understanding of what is essential in life for us to grow and prosper. The knowledge we can take from the First Nations' culture, enables us to relate it to our lives now and build a strong and ethical framework to underpin how we approach our practice and ensure we place the value of communities at the forefront of our work.

The Blackfoot framework considers the individual as deeply rooted within the community and the importance of shared learning across generations is vital. Intergenerational learning ensures that knowledge from past generations is passed down and that the next generation are then able to continue to hand over this knowledge to future generations. In Cindy Blackstock's "The emergence of the Breath of Life theory" (2011) she explains: "First Nations often consider their actions in terms of the impacts of the 'seven generations'. This means that one's actions are informed by the experience of the past seven generations and by considering the consequences for the seven generations to follow." In order to create environments where skills, care of one another and a mutual respect are exchanged so that individuals can reach their full potential, we need to move away from a triangle of need (as in Maslow's hierarchy) where we strive for the top of the pyramid and instead adopt Blackfoot's circular flow that recognises that our needs change order. Adopting this approach, community actualisation and community continuity is placed above self-actualisation. We all need to flourish in order for our society to be a happy, productive and prosperous space. The old phrase "No man is an island" taken from John Donne's poem ([1624]1988) reminds us that none of us are truly self-sufficient and that we need the comfort and companionship of others in order to thrive.

In Western society, where we prioritise Maslow's hierarchy of needs we put ourselves before others. Blackstock's Breath of Life theory (2011) identifies four domains for personal and collective growth: cognitive; social; emotional; and spiritual. That sense of integrated care and learning is evident within the Blackfoot culture and is one that can support us in the shaping and design of programmes for intergenerational practice. We must see emotional and intellectual needs as interdependent and create a space for shared community continuity where we can grow in all areas of our holistic development, across all of the generations.

Intergenerational care

Intergenerational care is when shared settings are provided to bring together younger and older generations. This could be through nursery and residential care provided on the same site or shared space for community day centres. Although growing in popularity across the globe, this is not a new concept. Shimada Masaharu merged a nursery and care home in Tokyo back in 1976 and since then the design of eldercare and daycare co-locations have gained popularity in their appeal to communities. The focus on intergenerational care is on the relationships built across generations and bridging the gap between young and old. The ability to co-locate care locations can bring great benefit to all generations and will lead to intergenerational learning taking place, through the array of activities and programmes that are undertaken between the two groups.

Intergenerational spaces are growing in popularity across the United Kingdom and for good reason. The UFAA's "The next generation" (2019) document highlights that by children spending time in intergenerational spaces, their language development will improve, social interactions will lead to positive attitudes towards ageing, and wellbeing will be boosted. In turn, older people will gain opportunities to spend time with others and this provides us with the opportunity to tackle social isolation and loneliness. A report "Care homes and intergenerational practice" undertaken by the organisation Linking Generations (2021) identified that, by bringing generations together, the social interaction had a multitude of health benefits for older people, including a potential reduced risk of dementia and physical problems such as high blood pressure, arthritis and cardiovascular conditions. A study in Japan by Morita and Kobayashi (2013) found that when elderly people were engaged in intergenerational care sessions, they were not only smiling and engaging more during the time they spent with the children, but that it also led to more engagement with one another as a result of the experience. Furthermore, residents felt more confident to strike up new conversations with each other and it gave them something new to talk about. It is not just the older participants that benefit, and Age UK highlight the co-located nursery and care home *Apples and Honey Nightingale* as leaders in the field for intergenerational care within the United Kingdom. The nursery found children benefited from listening to older residents' stories, developed their responsibility skills through their consideration of others and felt part of a long line of belonging. Nurseries are starting to use this evidence to inform their own practice, and we are seeing an increasing number of nurseries and care homes connecting throughout the year for social sessions. As we progress through this book you will be able to read a number of case studies from educators, and all found the social experiences just as enhancing as the educational ones.

Co-locating childcare and eldercare does not just bring with it social and emotional benefits. In 2021, Massachusetts Senate President Karen Spilka announced her focus on supporting women in the workforce as part of her post-pandemic recovery plans (Mass Live, 2021). One of the suggestions for working towards this was through strengthening intergenerational care options so that women were not overburdened with the care arrangements many of them manage for their children and older family members. By rethinking the approach to how care facilities were designed, Karen Spilka voiced that this would support the physical, emotional and public health outcomes in the long term. Policy makers are seeing the benefits of integrated models, and it is in everybody's interest to invest in building societies where we address needs using a holistic approach.

Intergenerational learning

We see intergenerational learning on a daily basis. A parent sitting down to support their child with their homework and the child sharing new techniques with them as parents share their knowledge to support the learning process. Grandparents sharing stories from their past experiences and children relating back their experiences from now. A shopkeeper counting out the change to a child and the child sharing some insight into what they have been learning at school. This informal learning provides a great benefit to children's knowledge and gives them a deeper understanding of adults' experiences and life. Both parties are engaged in mutual learning through an informal mechanism that comes from communicating and taking the time to listen to one another.

Intergenerational learning should incorporate the learning expectations of both children and adult attendees, in an inclusive and mutually beneficial space. It does not need to be held in a formal, traditional learning environment, but the sessions should have clear educational outcomes and be purposeful in their approach and delivery. In order to implement intergenerational learning, it is important for the lead educator on the project to define how the sessions will create spaces for children and older generations to strengthen the respect for one another and both gain something of value from their attendance and participation. It is not the lead educator's responsibility to come up with these outcomes independently but instead, to ensure that the planning will benefit all of the participants in attendance.

Intergenerational learning is a wonderful opportunity for older generations to pass down their knowledge to children. It also provides a mutually beneficial time for children to teach the adults they are with. By developing intergenerational learning, where all have the freedom to be heard and are respected for what they have to share, a deeper connection and respect for the project will mature. Relationships are key to a successful programme and by maintaining this as a value of your practice, you will find that your pupils' confidence will develop and greater engagement will come from feeling secure and encouraged within the intergenerational environment.

The process of intergenerational learning allows us to see our curriculums in a new way. In order to bring learning to life, we can use others' experiences and knowledge to see and hear first-hand how things work. We are able to see the purpose of what we are being taught and understand how it fits into the real world. The mutual sharing of knowledge between generations also brings with it an important opportunity for pupils. The understanding that their knowledge is important is a key element in intergenerational learning and builds their self-esteem and gives them the space to formulate their ideas and present them to others. This may challenge their concepts, which allows them to analyse their understanding further with individuals who are bringing different perspectives. Being able to see something from another's point of view is so desperately needed for future generations in order to promote inclusivity, diversity and representation.

Our focus within this book is on intergenerational learning; however, this learning cannot take place without the co-existing intergenerational care relationships being built first. UFAA's "The next generation" report (2019) recommends that by 2023 there should be an extension to co-located care facilities from the current 40 sites across the UK to 500. Although we may not find ourselves in positions where we are able to work in fully immersed shared sites, we have the ability to open our doors and provide a collection of programmes to support intergenerational practice within our educational spaces. By providing these sessions or a long- or short-term basis, you have the ability to make a difference within your society and bring communities together. Children will be able to engage in learning activities that will support them in understanding a diverse mix of people and spend time with a generation that they might not currently know. We have an exciting journey ahead of us in bringing generations together, and this book will help you to reflect on how you can embed this creatively within your practice and become an intergenerational advocate.

Active listening

The skill of active listening is a key component of intergenerational learning. Relationships between generations are built on trust and understanding and we must ensure that those in attendance, whether young or old, have the opportunity to be heard and valued for their contributions. Intergenerational learning requires us, as educators, to let go of control and create an equal space for participants to explore ideas together, understand different approaches and be responsive to different needs. Through the evaluation of intergenerational projects, I have seen the benefits that active listening brings to children's learning and self-confidence. Older generations have the skills and life experience to give children the time they need to sit and "be". There is a lot to be said for having this focus on being in the moment and reflecting together on the activity in hand. You project will be successful if it is built on the voice and needs of its participants and if we listen to what everyone has to say. Both children and older people often find themselves marginalised within society and by adopting this approach within our sessions, we empower them to share with their wider society what is important to them and build on the skills needed to create better futures. Intergenerational learning will require you to be responsive and remove all egos from the experience. This is not us teaching at the front of the class and telling people what to do, but rather us listening and responding to the events that take place and connecting them to the educational outcomes which we hope to achieve.

Lifelong learning

Within the remit of schools and colleges, it is our responsibility to teach our children a love of learning and inspire them to become lifelong learners. We work tirelessly to show them the opportunities that learning brings and to share with one another knowledge and ideas. Yet, we forget that one of the key ways of showing children and young people the benefits of lifelong learning is by surrounding them with role models outside of the educational environment. Think of the opportunities on your doorstep of the individuals who could share their wisdom with your pupils. I have seen this first-hand through a variety of events. At a local science fair, I met a retired lady who I had spoken to many times at church. I did not know her background and found out at the science fair that her background was in physics. She volunteers across the country to show young people the fun that comes from a science career, teaching them different experiments and sharing with them the joy she had found from her work. She told me the volunteering was incredibly rewarding as she felt passionately about what she did and the fairs gave her the chance to pass on her own experience to others. It also gave her time to keep her skills up to date and continue to learn her field of study. In turn, young people were able to learn from her experience and see a role model who had been successful, someone "like them" who had made it in a senior position.

I obtained my degree through the Open University. One of the pleasures of studying this way was the diverse mix of individuals I had as peers. At the graduation ceremony, I was able to observe just how many people had returned to education post-retirement. Our working life does not define our being, and we see evidence of those who use their time in retirement to learn a new skill or to seek new knowledge. My own mother has embraced language learning in her retirement, studying Spanish informally each day using an online teaching app. This fresh and new experience has been possible due to more time available thanks to work now not being part of the daily routine. In turn, there is a tremendous amount of knowledge that can now be shared with others due to this education. My mother has developed in her ability to speak a new language and this can be shared informally with my children in our day-to-day routines, snowballing the learning across the generations.

The more we can relate to others who we think may be different to us, the more we are able to see the connections and respect one another. This science fair exchange brought so much to both sides and by reflecting on what skills others may have, it can complement the educational experiences of children and young people. Exchanges of knowledge can provide pupils with the opportunity to make sense of the purpose of learning and give them a focus on where they would like to progress in the future.

If we explore post-retirement learning, we will discover a treasure trove that can offer our children an insight into new possibilities. With this post-retirement learning in mind, it is important for us to take a moment to reflect on our own educational establishments and how open/closed they are for older generations to have the ability to learn within them. Do our Further Education and university communities provide sessions that are relevant to our older members of society or do they only focus on those who will provide economic gain in the future? Where do informal learning exchanges between our primary schools and senior organisations take place?

The need for intergenerational connections

In Edgar Villanueva's *Decolonizing Wealth* book (2018), Dana Arviso reflects on how the Native Communities in Cheyenne River Territory view poverty. She recalls:

> They told me they don't have a word for poverty… The closest thing that they had as an explanation for poverty was "to be without family". Being without family was unheard of within the River Territory. This foreign concept, that someone could be so isolated and without any sort of safety net, family or have a sense of kinship, would cause great suffering and they deemed this as poverty.
>
> (2018, p. 151)

I am not trying to minimise here the critical impact that financial poverty has on families – financial poverty is causing even further risks and isolation within the United Kingdom – but rather, I am highlighting the importance of recognising that poverty can be viewed in a manner of ways, for example financially, digitally, emotionally, and that we must reflect on how vitally important it is to tackle poverty in a holistic manner.

When interviewing Nuala O'Toole from the "Kindness Postbox" (a case study we will explore further in Chapter 2) she told me the story of an individual who had received a letter from a pupil in her local community through her project and it had been nine years since the person had received a call, visit or a letter through the door. She asked me: "Imagine that you want a bill to drop through the door just so you have some communication with the outside world? Imagine anyone wanting a phone bill to land? How lonely must you be for that?". It struck a chord with just how many of our senior members of our society are living in total isolation and the way in which poverty can be viewed not only as a financial hardship but also emotionally I was fortunate to see a photo of the individual with her letter later in the conversation, and to say her eyes were like magic would be an understatement; the delight sparkled out radiantly. As a society, we have a lot more to do. Your projects are taking a step in social action and providing a basis for us to connect and learn from one another.

The increase of urbanisation and changes to the labour market and shifts in work/life patterns see families moving further apart from one another. This has impacted on the amount of time children get to spend with their grandparents and extended family. The link between generations in families has adapted and many children do not have the opportunities to meet with them as frequently. As our routines and landscapes change, we see our cities and towns growing bigger, with more and more of us moving to areas with economic and social opportunities. As this happens, our rural areas can become forgotten, and infrastructures will be prioritised by governments within cities rather than links for villages and more isolated locations. Many of our older generations live within these rural spots and find themselves unable to access social activities due to the lack of transportation and services close to home. Our countryside locations are filled with individuals who used to work the land and led active lives. Their lives may have consisted of quite isolated existences but their work and lifestyle could still have led to a fulfilled and happy routine. As individuals feel less physically able to participate in active life and retire from their rural jobs, there can be a lack of ability to interact with other people. Rural jobs still exist and we need our children and young people who will be handed down these vocational roles to feel that it will bring them a positive future. We need to build infrastructures within our rural communities that connects us and does not forget those on the outskirts.

It is not just within rural locations where individuals can feel fragmented from their community. People can feel just as isolated within busy cities as they can within our rural locations across societies. Scharf and De Jong Gierveld (2008) discuss how unsafe and deprived neighbourhoods in big cities are highly exposed to increased feelings of isolation and loneliness. The cost of living is increased, leading to difficulties in accessing social activities, so many older individuals find themselves confined within the walls around them. Social isolation is increased by urbanisation and economic focus. We have a civic duty to work for the greater good of our society and to make sure that children not only get the educational experiences to which they have a right, but also have prospects available to them within their immediate environment. There is not an area across Western society where intergenerational connections should not be prioritised and we all have the ability to make a direct difference to our local area by taking social action and embedding intergenerational activities into our educational systems.

2 Moving beyond an annual carol service

Intergenerational events are common in schools and other educational establishments. As the year progresses, festivals and traditions remind us of our civic duty to be kind to others and help where we can. I remember the Harvest Festival well: tins of food donations brought in to share with our elderly neighbours and those in need, we sang songs, said our prayers and teachers visited the different local residents and organisations to pass on our collection.

The harvest collection continues in many schools today, and we see wonderful events organised throughout the year to link with our senior citizens. Intergenerational learning is a pedagogy of practice though that shifts these activities to an educational experience and we need to recognise that there is more to underpin the events than an annual trip to a local care home. This is not to belittle that work; for many schools, their commitment to organising choirs to sing for care home residents or to send in artwork for them to enjoy is a step in the right direction in teaching children the values of kindness and doing things for others. However, if you want to be a leader in intergenerational practice then you need to move away from this mindset and evaluate how we can extend these activities to design them in a way that is mutually beneficial and directly relates to the educational outcomes that we have identified to be delivered through intergenerational activities. We have explored the differences in embedding intergenerational practice in your provision and it is important for us to recognise the importance of an equal learning experience between the different generations. This can be challenging for educators as our focus has always been predominately on children and young people so it will help you to collaborate with your counterparts from the care sector to reflect on how you do this effectively.

Intergenerational practice is not a one-off event. Of course, benefits can come from visits to local care homes, organising concerts and celebratory days for seniors within your community. However, when implementing intergenerational practice it should be embedded into your action plans and approached with a clear purpose and vision for collaborative working. By using creative thinking and innovative techniques, children have the opportunity to learn from adults through a vast number of experiences and knowledge exchange sessions. These opportunities allow you to deliver pupils' curriculums with rich and seasoned activities, which engage the individual and build on the communication skills of the children and young people with whom you are working.

For those of us who are not within leadership roles, it is important to work in partnership with our managers to review the settings policies and reflect on how they support intergenerational learning. If it does not fit within our policies and development plan then it can be difficult to justify and overcome barriers to introducing intergenerational learning into our provision. If you are on the journey of your initial designs of an intergenerational project, you may find that by reviewing the policies initially and putting together an evidence-informed proposal will support you when presenting this to the leaders within your provision. By paying attention to the detail from the outset you will be able to gain an investment from all involved as they will see a purpose to your intentions.

Your plans for your intergenerational programmes should be built on the needs of the children and young people we work with, alongside those who join you to participate. We need to move away from intergenerational sessions being a tokenistic add-on to curriculums and instead one that forms a natural part of our learning schedule. The World Health Organization (Centre for Ageing Better, 2021) includes respect and social inclusion in one of its eight domains for building and sustaining age-friendly communities, and projects such as this help us to support the development of community links and create a mutual respect across generations. For intergenerational learning to be effective we need to focus on relationships first and create opportunities for bonds to be made. Planning for this stage is vital and there are a number of steps that can be incorporated to support attendees in getting to know one another and form the relationships so vitally important for a successful programme of events.

When I was working on our first intergenerational programme, the team considered together whom we would invite from the senior community. Local care homes were important to us as they were places we walked past every day but (in most cases) did not tend to engage with. Older people were on one side of the wall and we were on the other. It was crucial for us to make this link and to work with people who we had not had the opportunity to meet in everyday circumstances. We started the process with older students visiting the centre with their teachers and introducing themselves. They explained about the project that we had designed and then sat to discuss it further over a cup of tea and biscuits. There is a lot to be said for a cup of tea, and over the years we have had many of our most moving conversations with others in this way. It has given us the opportunity to find out more about why people would like to sign up and hear first-hand the barriers as to why they feel they may not be able to participate. These conversations allowed us to revisit our plans and adapt them to ensure we adopted an inclusive approach to our practice. For those of you working with younger children, you may want to consider how play-based activities could support children to get to know residents. The use of video calls, letter exchanges and your usual activities such as the harvest collection could be a means for reviewing how you can build on these to make it a sustainable project throughout the year.

When visiting the care homes, we quickly learnt that when we were explaining the project to the main group, not all of the residents could hear us very well and also did not feel confident asking questions whilst we were speaking. It was during this time that we learnt the importance of touch and close conversations, something we often shy away from in education. Yorkston et al. (2012) explain that as we get older, our communication skills diminish and this leads to life consequences such as avoiding social situations. This is one of the reasons it is so vitally important to create spaces where we feel at ease and safe together, clearly explaining our intentions. Older people would lean into us to hear, take our hand as we spoke and looked directly at us as we engaged in conversation. The feedback from students on this was very interesting and all of us found it very different to what we were used to. We all found it a special experience to engage with people in this way and found that it brought a connection that reminded us of time spent with grandparents and older relatives who were important to us. It brought new relationships that would form the basis of our programme and gave us the opportunity to completely engage in the moment, not distracted by the next task or the technology around us.

It had been some time for me since I had enjoyed these types of conversations with my own grandmothers and I realised instantly how much I missed it. The calming aura of their concentration and their time to commit to the true art of conversation made a real impact on our emotional health, an area so vitally important for us to be concentrating on with our children and young people. Students had no choice but to engage in what was in front of them, and the kindness and attention from both parties was an incredibly rewarding area to observe.

It was during these sessions that the residents decided if they wanted to join us – and this in itself is something we must be aware of when we are planning our activities: not everyone will want to come! If we go into this as an *instructor* with no focus on relationship building then we will not have people engaging in the programme that we hope to run. I have seen it so many times throughout my life where, as people get older, people begin to speak to them as if they were children. I challenge this approach on both sides of the coin. Children are more than capable of making their own decisions through developmentally appropriate informed choice, adults most certainly are as well! We need to stop infantilising senior members of our community, a trait common within the UK discourse of ageing. Ego needs to be stripped back completely when engaging in intergenerational practice and we need to actively listen to what everyone has to say, not provide commands on what will happen next.

When running any type of intergenerational programme, it is important for that shift to take place in the way in which we communicate with children, young people and senior people within our community. As a trained Early Years Educator, I spend much of my time talking to very young children and see how well they respond and enjoy complex conversations, where they are introduced to new vocabulary and are able to make informed decisions through the discussions that we have. We tend to speak to those we see as vulnerable differently to how we communicate with the rest of our peers and sometimes subconsciously find ourselves talking down to senior people and children, infantilising language and conversations as we engage. This can often be a subconscious act and one that is very important to recognise in order for us to empower those with which we work and spend time with. Talking "at" people will not help in building the important relationships on which intergenerational projects are based. Throughout your projects, the art of active listening and complete engagement in the activities you are running is **so** vital to ensure people feel secure and confident within the space. When having conversations with those who may have dementia, hearing impairments or other needs, the importance of time to converse must be high on your agenda and this is one of the reasons why exploring the best texts, activities and group activities is important for how you approach your sessions. During a reading exchange programme where students read books online for attendees at a local care home (reviewed further in Chapter 6), we made it very clear to students that it did not matter if they stumbled over words or got lost within the page. What mattered was their commitment to being brave and sharing their voice with others. This not only boosted their confidence but saw them highly engaged as they could see the purpose and were heavily involved in leading their learning. In turn, this supported us in developing their public speaking and reading skills in a safe and encouraging environment.

In the intergenerational projects in which I have been involved, I have been lucky to collaborate with care homes that are leaders in their field and work from an ethics of care, understanding their residents' needs whilst actively listening to what they say and what they want. In one of the independent living homes which we worked with, some residents did not want to attend our sessions. Some had busy routines that meant our event clashed with their own plans and others just did not want to participate as they were content in their current routine. We agreed we would not question them as to why; they had their own reasons and I hope they knew that they had an open invitation if they ever changed their mind. There was no pressure and no animosity and for those who did sign up to participate we knew that we were committed to them and vice versa. Those that did join us understood before attending the expectations from all sides and had already begun to build relationships with the older students and us (the teachers). For those working with younger children, it may not be possible for the children to meet with the senior adults before their first session with you. This was the case in some of our projects as our focus was on the further education students and we had limited time with pupils from the primary school. We needed to consider the layout of our environment and, as we created a space that brought both teenage and primary-age children together, we reflected on how we could have a mix of the teens and senior participants who have already started to build on their relationships, scattered accordingly with the children from the primary school. We met with the primary teachers responsible for the groups prior to the programme and considered how we could best place children within the environment for active conversations and also reviewed the activities we could design in order to prompt conversations to get to know one another. We wanted this to be a fun, learning experience for everyone and analysed how we would be able to create that from the outset.

We adapted our seating plans depending on the groups that would visit us. Ideally we hoped for it to be child – adult – child seated around the table but due to primary class sizes we were not always able to have a balance of groups of the same size from each generation. We also had to consider that not all of the older attendees felt comfortable without a companion to sit with them initially so we adapted it to suit their preferences. Having more children was not a problem as we found that having small groups participating in round table-top activities allowed for plenty of discussion.

It is important for us to work with the care workers from the nursing home who attend our sessions with senior participants and to be flexible in our approach to the programmes so that we could accommodate everybody's hopes and needs for the session. In order to develop the relationships between the adults and children, within each of our programmes we tried to maintain the same seating plan so that the bond between adults and children could form and continue over each of the visits. If a child or adult was poorly or unable to attend then this would be noted by the other parties and we had to explain why someone was not in attendance! By using a table group, we were able to support the development of relationships between all those seated together, and a valuable bond came from all those sitting within each space. You may find that as your programmes evolve then you may wish your children and young people to get to know more of the attendees, so reflect on when and how this is going to be most beneficial for all participants.

As our own programme expanded, we began to work with care homes with people from all different age groups. The care homes supported those with learning disabilities and for some of the attendees, a new environment could become overwhelming. It was vitally important to work with the care homes to ensure that everyone was safe and secure and we did not leave anyone in a vulnerable position. This was a wonderful progression of our programme as it saw further attendees engaging in our programmes who often found themselves isolated from many social activities. We had to plan the seating arrangements differently in this situation and they sat at a table alongside the children and senior attendees for the first half of the year with their chaperones. Children would build relationships slowly by sharing some of their artwork and observing one another. It led to opportunities for children to spend time with those with learning disabilities in an environment that celebrated differences and an understanding that we can all learn and enjoy social time together. As you progress within intergenerational practice, you will find yourself reviewing how to develop further connections with your community due to the benefits that have come from your engagement with others.

During the initial sessions we reviewed activities that we could do which enabled the groups to get to know one another. We were aware that some of the adults found it difficult to hold pens or pencils therefore we tried to move away from this during activities so that our practice did not embarrass any of the attendees or leave an impact on their own self-esteem. It was also important for us as educators to move around the tables to give guidance on the session, as speaking from a distance made it difficult for those with hearing impairments to hear us. Moving from space to space also ensured that we could check in with both adults and children to confirm their understanding of the activities that we had laid out. Consider during your sessions the physical needs of your participants and what you can do to make it a comfortable and enjoyable experience. Preparation is key and alongside verbal instructions you may find it beneficial to also leave out a note on each table of what you have planned in both written and pictorial labelling so that both adults and children can understand how to complete the activities that you have planned. This ensures that the tasks do not cause any distress or confusion to any of the attendees.

Reflect on how short activities can snowball into connections and educational experiences. The following case studies will provide an understanding of how others have been able to develop this through community links.

The "Kindness Postbox" case study

Nuala O'Toole: "I only went out for a cup of tea."

I was introduced to Nuala through the organisation Linking Generations after they told me Nuala was someone I had to meet due to her inspirational intergenerational work during the Covid-19 lockdown period. As soon as I got on the Zoom call to chat about the kindness project, I was inspired by her energy, innovation and consideration of others. Nuala's project shows us how one-off events can ripple out to intergenerational learning and social exchanges and enhance the experiences for all those involved.

When the lockdown period was announced, Nuala was told that she would have to shield, leaving her isolated from her usual social network. Realising the importance of interactions for her health and wellbeing, Nuala put all of her energy into creating links within her community to bring together different generations. A postbox was placed in her local convenience shop where children could leave post that would be collected later in the week and delivered to some of the local nursing homes. Starting with a small initial collection, the project has now grown with hundreds of letters delivered weekly across Northern Ireland with schools, colleges and local community groups participating in the exchange. Her work has rippled out, with local charities such as "Men's Shed" building the postboxes for local schools and councils have contacted Nuala to gain an insight into how they can meet with their commitments to tackling social isolation.

Through the Kindness Postbox, Nuala is surrounded by children's creations on a weekly basis. She has an array of letters and drawings that she can put her hand to as we talk. The letters are handled with love and care, with an awareness of the impact these letters will have on individuals once they are received. Nuala also mentions the positive impact it has had being surrounded by the beautiful colours and creativity. She believes that being surrounded by this has had a very positive impact on her own emotional wellbeing and there is a sense of spirituality through the gift of sharing such bright and caring images with others.

Nuala is an incredibly humble individual. She makes it very clear that the project is easy to set up and discusses how it helped her during a difficult time. She runs the project with Wendy and Michelle and it is evident that all three gain a great deal from running the Kindness Postbox, meeting for weekly tea and cake whilst they make their deliveries to the care homes. Although Nuala does not credit her commitment, it is due to her passion and drive that it has become such a success. The temporary postboxes have become a permanent feature in many spaces across the community. I came away from the interview with Nuala feeling pure joy and inspiration (alongside signing up to set up a postbox with the students I work with!), and it was a reminder of how values and passion are key to the success of implementing intergenerational work.

I asked about the barriers to the project and it is Nuala's positive mindset that allows her to see past these. Barriers do not feature in her work; instead she seeks solutions and works proactively with her local community to find people who will help her. Nuala is a good people reader and knows when someone is not interested, moving on to find someone who does want to help. In order to maintain the growth of the project, she has had to learn new skills such as designing websites, creating spreadsheets to store information and collaborating with local councils and organisations that work in this area to represent the people with whom she is connecting. It is making ripples of change and those in the position of policy and budget-making decisions are recognising the importance of social action projects such as the Kindness Postbox. People want to talk to Nuala because she is on the ground making a difference; she recognises that for change to happen you need to step forward.

I have no hesitation in saying that it is Nuala's determination for the project to succeed, and actively getting out into her community, that has made this project grow so quickly and purposefully. As the project has progressed they have been able to connect with more senior people living independently, and there are now transportable postboxes which can be collected whilst volunteers are out and about. Letters are reviewed before they get sent out and there are templates so that permissions are granted for any photos or creations to be shared both with individuals and online, using the Kindness Postbox website and social media pages. To allow for connections back and forth, contact names are provided, so that a relationship can be formed through the letter exchange, and for those senior members who are unable to write, the care home activity coordinators write a collective response to capture this communication. Nuala has seen what a difference this project has made and tells me about an individual who has not received a visit, phone call or piece of post for nine years. When I see a photo of the person with their post I am overwhelmed; it captures the sparkle in the eye and the most radiant smile.

Nurseries, schools and colleges engage on a regular basis and see the benefits for children and young people of connecting in this way and are also able to relate it to the curriculum that they are following. Children are able to develop their literacy skills through their writing, ICT skills and creativity, alongside feeling a greater sense of belonging within their environment.

As we end our first conversation (and one that is the first of many), Nuala explains that all she wanted was a reason to go out for a cup of tea. Once the project got off the ground she and Wendy said they channelled "Thelma and Louise" and hit the road delivering letters across County Fermanagh. Nuala has made a sustainable project where she clearly drives what happens but also has brought in a range of individuals as a support network to keep the project alive, continually responding to the creativity of ideas and the needs of local people. Some schools want permanent links, some of the local supermarkets want to participate on a short-term scale. The plans are kept simple in order to accommodate different needs. As I reflect on my meeting with Nuala, I realise she is everything I aspire to be: kind, radiant, proactive and determined. We all need to be more Nuala and step up to make a change.

Inspiration from the "Kindness Postbox" project

Nuala's personality makes you feel instantly engaged and inspired to make changes after speaking with her. During one of our telephone conversations, I asked her if we could set up our own project within the college using her Kindness Postbox project, and half an hour later I received a wealth of resources from Nuala that gave me real practical information as to how to set it up and make it a success. I reflected on our own remit and how we could get the most from the project for students. Like all of our college projects, the most important people to share this thinking with were the students and we explored together how this could benefit their learning and sense of purpose. We also considered our skills and expertise, evaluating how we could develop the project to work within the college environment. Following several years of delivering intergenerational projects on site that were led by the students, I worked with a Year 1 group who would be with us for the next two years, so that they could see this as their focus of building relationships within their community before progressing to delivering face-to-face sessions on site later on in their qualification.

Many of Nuala's postboxes attract countless letters from younger children, a real treat to receive, but we decided our main aim would be to promote the postbox within the college across all curriculum areas in order to get letters from mainly teenage students and from the lecturers and staff who work within the organisation. For us, the values of connection, community and kindness underpinned what we were trying to do within this social action project.

This project had come up quite quickly and I was aware that both the students and I were committed to many other areas of focus so it was important for us to recognise this and collaborate with others across the college in order to make it a success. When planning for any type of intergenerational project it is important for us to recognise our capacity and actively seek out those who can help us. We recognised the importance of connecting with senior members of our society through our research. Age UK (2018) have highlighted that 400,000 people over the age of 65 worry about being lonely at Christmas, with over half of those over 75 living alone and 5 million saying that their only companion is a television. We were deeply aware that many would be feeling isolated over the Christmas holidays and we could take a positive step to bring some connection.

An email that had come earlier in the week from our Enterprise Coordinator gave me the opportunity to seek help for the project outside of our curriculum area. Within a week he had helped us to build our own postbox by approaching the joinery team and asking them to build one for us using recycled materials from their department. He also shared some ideas on how we could extend the project through links with external organisations and helped us to plan it with a cross-campus approach. His skillset was of great benefit to us. If I had tried to do this independently it would have been a lengthy process, to which I would not have been able to commit. You may not have someone within your organisation who is dedicated to starting up projects in the same way; however, there is an array of individuals who are usually happy to help (and have it as part of their remit), who can bring something that we ourselves do not have to offer. Sometimes it can help to look outside your own organisation, to consider how collaborations can support your intergenerational work or to meet as a team to evaluate the skills and interests of the team. Sometimes that conversation can surprise us and we can discover that colleagues have skills we were not previously aware of.

Over a two-month period we had been able to build a sustainable project that would not just be a one-off Christmas event but instead something that we could build into our daily culture within the college, and we continue to follow up with newsletter articles, sharing of photographs of residents receiving their letters and collecting letters returned to students and staff from the care homes. The learning from the letter exchanges may not be specific to the students' curriculum content but enriches their lives and shows that others care and thus forms the basis for later projects in which they will participate. This particular project started as one for us to connect with residents with the view of later inviting them in for other programmes, but it has also led to the building of a culture where intergenerational practice is very much part of the day-to-day life of students and staff and is visible for others to see. This supports us in showcasing the benefits of intergenerational learning and encourages others to become involved.

Vicki Titterington from the organisation Linking Generations offers some advice on this type of activity within educational settings and explains that we do not have to do this as an add-on activity but instead should consider how what we are currently doing can be shifted so that it can be done in a new way that connects us with our communities. When children do some artwork for Christmas, why not have this as a piece that can be distributed to local care homes? Christmas baubles with a special message of hope can be sent as gifts to those within our community. She also recommends turning your activities into sustainable projects; rather than just sending out cards at Christmas, review what other key dates you could use for distributing letters. Moving letter exchanges from once a year to once a quarter can provide your pupils with a valuable connection to their local community.

3 Global approaches to intergenerational practice

Loneliness is on the agenda of many Governments across the globe, and there are numerous factors that can lead to why individuals do not feel integrated into the society in which they live. Recreational spaces, local amenities, social activities and access to services can all lead to negative experiences if we do not have the ability to access these areas in a safe and comfortable manner. In 2021, the World Health Organization (WHO) published their first global report on the impact of ageism. It outlined a framework, with clear recommendations on what could be done within societies to prevent and tackle ageism. Their report made it clear that if ageism features within communities then we are unable to take full advantage of people's skills and talents, a disadvantage for society as a whole. Ageism is a huge factor in social isolation and discrimination. The report (WHO, 2021) identified that one in two people are ageist towards older people. With this shockingly high number, we clearly need to do more within societies to stop this form of discrimination within our communities.

The WHO highlighted three areas that could be used to combat ageism: policy and law, educational activities, and intergenerational activities. With educational activities seen as the most effective strategy, we have an advantage within education to make this a key priority on our agendas and make a difference to the lives of our senior members of society. The European Commission (2018) highlighted that in Europe we are living longer but more often alone, leading to an increase in loneliness and isolation within our societies due to our ageing population. The pandemic of 2020 further increased feelings of isolation and loneliness, leaving many vulnerable individuals finding it difficult to reintegrate into social situations after being alone for a long period of time. Globally, social isolation and loneliness of our older generations are very much on the agenda, and many policies and strategies are being implemented to try to tackle this problem and reduce the number of people feeling isolated.

In 2021 the Fondazione Giacomo Brodolini and the European Centre for Social Welfare Policy and Research found that social isolation had a greater impact on older people than on any other age group across Europe. Within countries such as the United Kingdom and France there have been national strategies that focus on combating loneliness in older people. Additionally, there have also been many programmes that have been designed at a community

DOI: 10.4324/9781003262688-4

level. These grassroot projects have brought great change and worked effectively to bring generations together. We should strive to learn from both policies and programmes in order to design diverse and dynamic spaces that allow us to connect and share our experiences across generations.

The Jo Cox Commission on Loneliness (2017) produced a report that provided a strategic approach on how to tackle loneliness in the United Kingdom. In response to this report the UK Government implemented a Minister to be responsible for civil society and in 2018 a UK-wide strategy was appointed to address loneliness. Initially the Jo Cox Commission was to run for one year, bringing 13 organisations together to highlight the scale of loneliness across the United Kingdom; however, following the report and the appointment of a new Minister for Loneliness, the Government put into place the "Connected society strategy" (Department for Digital, Culture, Media and Sport [DDCMS], 2018) with a key priority of building community infrastructures that empowers social connections. By utilising spaces, including schools and green spaces, the Government evaluated how they could build on how we connect a diverse range of people together within them. The #IWill movement (www.iwill.org.uk) was launched from this strategy which aimed to inspire young people to get involved in social action and make a difference within their communities. For one of our own intergenerational projects undertaken within the college, we reached the final stages of the Association of Colleges Beacon Award in conjunction with #IWill, and our emphasis on students taking the lead for creating change and making a difference within our society was recognised, an important milestone for highlighting to students the value of their work and the recognition outside of our own organisation.

The DDCMS Strategy (2018) also set priorities to create a societal shift in order to tackle social isolation effectively and pledged to build a culture that supported connected communities through helping grassroot projects and building a national campaign to raise awareness and reduce the stigma surrounding loneliness. Within the paper, Nick Gibb, who was the Minister of State for School Standards at the time, was recorded as highlighting the role that intergenerational learning had in addressing loneliness and valuing community obligations. This is an important statement as it shows us, as educators, the importance of embedding intergenerational opportunities within our curriculums and ensures that the strategies priorities are met.

The four Nations across the United Kingdom have implemented a number of initiatives to tackle social isolation within their countries, both at grassroots and Governmental level. In 2017 MSP Christine Grahame raised a motion within the Scottish Parliament to highlight the importance of intergenerational practice within educational settings (Generations Working Together, 2017). From visiting projects she observed the connection between nursery children and older attendees and she remarked on how these opportunities benefited children's physical development alongside offering a new way to develop their emotional and social needs. Her hope was for further nurseries and care homes to come together in order to replicate what she had seen and, in turn, she highlighted the work of the "Generations Working Together" charity. This was key for the Government and voluntary organisations collaborating together in order to tackle social isolation and focus on intergenerational practice as a means of supporting societal change.

The motion met with a positive response and Elaine Smith recognised the impact of social isolation on people's lives, highlighting that within Scottish society over two hundred thousand older people go half a week or more with no visitors or phone calls from anyone. The opportunity to bring young and old together was identified as a way to show older people that they are valued and that there are many who want to listen to their stories. By Christine Grahame securing the debate within the Scottish Government chamber there was an opportunity to bring intergenerational practice to the forefront of policy makers' minds and key priority areas. It has since led to Scotland designing policies and programmes to tackle social isolation and connect generations.

2020 saw Wales launch their first strategy on tackling social isolation and loneliness. The strategy had four priority areas: increasing opportunities for people to connect; building community infrastructure that supports connected communities; cohesive and supportive communities; and building awareness and promoting positive attitudes. The Welsh Government adopted a strategic approach (2020) to reflect on how they could support society in developing what was needed in order for people to feel safe and connected to their local environment. There was an awareness within the publication that the Government could not make changes overnight and in the short term it could lead to statistically more loneliness being recorded within evaluations due to people recognising themselves as isolated through their interactions with the campaign. However, they recognised the opportunity to invest in the future and 1.4 million pounds was allocated over a three-year cycle through this strategy to test out innovative strategies for tackling loneliness and social isolation. The commitment to trying something new was a brave step and an important mechanism for connecting with grassroot projects.

During the lockdown period of 2020, research was undertaken at a collaborative level across Northern Ireland leading to the publication of "Loneliness in Northern Ireland: A Call to Action" (Quinn, 2020). To date, Northern Ireland has not implemented a nationwide strategy to tackle social isolation and loneliness, leaving it the only country within the United Kingdom without one. The aim of this publication was to use evidence-based campaigning to inform the local Government of what society needed in a strategy to move forward. One of the strategies presented within the book is to map the existing services and recognise the positive work that is already being done in this area. By identifying the work, this may be developed further using a collaborative design across all levels. It was also a beneficial step to have this completed during the lockdown period as it allowed for a review of the impact this had had on society and shape policy in line with this as the country moved forward.

Although Northern Ireland does not have its own strategy, the "Age friendly network" was launched in 2019 in partnership with the Department for

Communities and the Public Health Agency (AgeNI, 2019). The aim of this network was to support the 11 councils across Northern Ireland to advance age-friendly planning and practices. This has led to councils prioritising their age-friendly agenda and connecting with the projects within communities that lead on intergenerational experiences. All four Nations (Northern Ireland, Scotland, Wales and England) and the Republic of Ireland have prioritised tackling social isolation and loneliness in some manner and this gives us scope to prioritise intergenerational learning within our education systems and to widen the experiences that we can offer to children, young people and the wider community.

Intergenerational learning and care are not just on the agenda within the United Kingdom; indeed many countries have embedded it into their community and education systems. In fact, it is not a new approach as this has been implemented effectively in Tokyo since the seventies (as discussed in Chapter 2) and has since gained world-wide attention. Traditionally in Japan, elderly parents would live with their eldest son, and similarly to Europe they have found that there has been a decrease in three-generation households and more senior members of society are faced with isolation and loneliness. Intergenerational care in Japan has been seen as a way of tackling this and giving generations more opportunity to spend time together. Tokyo currently now has 16 intergenerational facilities where childcare and eldercare is co-located, with more models of co-existing edu/eldercare centres on the horizon.

Singapore has also set key priorities to design more intergenerational facilities in order to further bring people together. New developments are underway for eldercare and childcare facilities to be on the same site and in turn bring opportunities for older and younger people to spend time together and learn together. In 2018 Singapore opened its first intergenerational playground and the childcare centre that was co-located within a nursing home facility was accessible to everyone. The senior Minister of State for Health described the playground as a trailblazer amongst nursing homes where the universal concept of play was recognised as a need for both the young and old. With loneliness regarded as one of the greatest health risks for older people (Holt-Lunstad et al. 2015) outdoor learning and community space is a highly beneficial way of bringing people together.

By creating this co-located space there was a hope that older people would gain more opportunities from the infectious energy of youth and that the young children would be more understanding of older people within their local area. This mutually beneficial approach is highly important in how we approach intergenerational practice. The playground was purposefully designed to support those with physical needs, and the play equipment was wheelchair accessible allowing all to experience the freedom of play. Alongside the playground other spaces were created that encouraged children and older people to spend time together in activities such as artwork and eating together. Redesigning the environmental barriers that once prevented participation allowed more active engagement, more physical movement and social circumstances that would otherwise not occur.

Across the globe we can see different strategies for building cohesive communities and in 2014, the Netherlands Department for Ministry of Health launched a "Reinforced action plan against loneliness" (Zolyomi, 2019). The purpose of this programme was to identify loneliness at an early stage and to bring the discussion of loneliness to the forefront of conversation. By creating an alliance of Government organisations, the voluntary sector and business partners together, there was an opportunity for a sustainable approach to tackling loneliness in Dutch communities.

The Dutch Government has continued to pledge financial and political aid to tackling social isolation. With 1.3 million people in the Netherlands over 75 years of age (Good News Network, 2021) the "One against loneliness" campaign was launched to encourage organisations, communities, businesses and individuals to find solutions to tackle loneliness at a local level. One of the major supermarket chains came up with their own idea for this and introduced the "chat checkout" with this now being a feature in 200 of their stores. The checkouts encourage their customers not to rush through the checkouts and instead stand for a chat with the staff as they pay for their goods. The company explained that although this is a small gesture, they wanted their stores to be more than just a grocery store and more of a community space. The "chat checkout" has led to further initiatives with some of their stores now introducing activities such as "chat corners" where coffee and a relaxing space are offered in order for people to come together and enjoy some time relaxing and engaging in conversation. The link between public, private and voluntary organisations collaborating together is a key tool required for building a community that cares for one another and appreciates others' skills and knowledge.

After a trip to see our granny one Saturday morning, I popped into her local grocery shop and saw first-hand what a hub of the community the local shops are. Living in a village on the outskirts of town, my life slowed down as I walked in. A young shop assistant was coming through the doors to help an older lady carry her shopping to the car, one of the aisles was blocked by a group of local residents catching up and I waited patiently to get the produce I needed before heading home. As I paid for my items, the person serving me took the time to chat and ask questions. I realised how much of a hurry I am usually in, and I really enjoyed the conversation. That morning, what I witnessed in the shop was much more than convenience, but rather it was a social space where people were able to connect and come to a place accessible to them to meet with others. Just like convenience stores, hairdressers, local cafés and banks can be a regular feature in elderly people's lives for connections with others. Throughout this chapter we have seen Governments identifying the need to connect with grassroot projects, and it is in building these spaces and Governments supporting them that we are able to build sustainable links within our communities to bring society together in order to tackle social isolation effectively.

Over the lockdown period of 2020/21, I intentionally started using our local stores as it gave me the opportunity to have a conversation with others. I dearly missed the daily interactions I would usually participate in, and doing a smaller shop locally allowed me to engage in at least some small conversations with someone outside of my family home. I was lucky. I had others to go home to and yet I still felt lonely at times as I missed my usual schedule. It was a stark reminder of how important it is for policy makers to take action to support those who feel socially isolated. As our high streets start to close down across the United Kingdom and independent stores decrease, we need to ensure there are initiatives in place that recognise what a lifeline these places can be for those feeling isolated and lonely.

In 2019, the French "MONALISA" programme, implemented by the then French Minister for older people and independent living to mobilise older people and provide a network to fight social isolation building on existing structures, had 287 teams registered who were trained specifically to tackle social isolation and the loneliness of older people. The teams identify older citizens within communities and support them with activities such as accompanying them on hospital trips or helping them in administrative tasks. During the Covid-19 pandemic the support offered was adjusted accordingly and responses to differing needs were put in place. This included more intense online communication to ensure that those isolated did not find themselves without anyone to talk to.

The French priority of supporting older community members has led to a number of initiatives being implemented. Through assistive technology, an app called "Snapmiam" was designed to connect older and younger generations. There was a recognition of the needs of the two age groups and "Snapmiam" offers a platform where students can find low-cost, healthy home-made meals made by older community members. The students go to eat the meals cooked by older people and these are enjoyed together. The app is a useful tool for tackling social isolation and bringing together two groups who would not normally spend time in each other's company. This is a highly beneficial and forward-thinking approach for intergenerational learning, where both groups gain something from the exchange. This sort of initiative is one where trust is integrated into the design and one we could consider as we approach intergenerational practice designs. Our fears can sometimes lead us to be overly cautious thereby missing opportunities to connect together.

Another French initiative is the "Yvelines Student Programme", where each summer 150 students are employed by their local council to collaborate with local social action centres. The students spend their summer months visiting socially isolated elderly people and participate in activities such as playing board games together, going for walks or visiting the hairdressers with their partner. The project has been in place since the French heatwave of 2003, where many older community members were unable to leave their home and has since had over 96,000 visits to older residents' homes. This programme shows the mutual benefit to both age groups: students are able to earn money during their summer holidays, gain experience and participate in rich dialogue with their older partner and the senior individual gains company, social time and support as they require.

A poll commissioned in America by Generations United and The Eisner Foundation (2018) found that nearly all Americans believed that children and older people have the skills and talents to help one another and that 85 per cent would prefer childcare and eldercare to be facilitated on a co-located site rather than in different buildings. America also values the importance of intergenerational practice and the Older American's Act (Kaplan et al. 2008) authorises funding for non-profit organisations to carry out intergenerational programmes and policies to actively promote intergenerational structures to be embedded into facilities for children and young people.

One of the fundamental reasons why there are not more co-located sites for childcare and eldercare is due to the red tape that governs our provision. I am not suggesting that the checks and protection mechanisms should not be in place but there does need to be more flexibility for educators to be able to be more innovative in their practice and shape facilities in line with research and the needs of those using their services. As an Early Years Educator, I have seen nursery settings struggle to design spaces where different age groups of children can come together, where children can be cared for alongside their older and younger siblings due to it not conforming with the guidelines for different age groups being cared for in separated spaces. Our policy makers need to make a commitment to removing the barriers we often find to supporting our communities and bringing people together within our educational and care models of practice. Our policy makers have set the priorities to build our societies in a mutually beneficial way and it is important for them to accept that adaptations need to be made to environments and policies in order for the work to take place.

Governments and policy makers are investing in intergenerational practice and this supports us as educators to link our programmes to outcomes for children, young people, older people and communities. Your work in this area is needed and by embedding an evidence-based approach, you will be able to identify how you are meeting a broad number of targets both within education and in the wider remit of society. The need for intergenerational care and education is being recognised on a global scale and we have seen throughout this chapter how grassroot projects have influenced policy makers' approaches to designing strategies. Throughout my own research I have observed how small projects ripple out to make a difference and the interest it makes to those in positions who focus on community development. Our work in bringing generations together is not just an add-on to enhance the learning environment but a key priority across the world and a priority for the values that we hold to create better communities for our children and young people to grow within.

4 Building societies where all generations come together

Our educational establishments are not often built with the intention of hosting the wider community in which it is located. Child-size tables and chairs, playgrounds with nothing but tarmac, and busy corridors can make it difficult to welcome a group of older visitors into our provision. Our community spaces are similar. Next time you take a walk around your town or village, take note of the distance between places to sit, how wide the pavement path is and how easy it is to cross a road in a safe space. If you had physical or sensory impairment, would your community be an easy place in which to travel confidently? Senior members of our society often struggle with these barriers, leading to them staying at home more. This in turn, leads to less confidence to go out into the community and further deterioration in their physical capabilities. As we find ourselves in a health and social care crisis in the United Kingdom, we need to work much harder at supporting people in their independence and emotional wellbeing. We know that physical factors impact on bringing communities together, and this puts the onus on us to reflect on how we can make our own spaces open, connected and friendly to all those we hope will feel safe and secure within them.

The current health and social care crisis

In 1948 the National Assistance Act was introduced in order to ensure that assistance was given to everybody who needed it over 16 years of age, including those who were unable to make National Insurance contributions. This was when we saw what is described as the "Welfare State" introduced within the United Kingdom, where the Government is responsible for its citizens' individual and social welfare. Although there was some emphasis on social welfare prior to this, for example within the first Elizabethan age and poor law and workhouse legislations, this is where we find a turning point for how the Government is held to account for the welfare of societies through legislation. During the 1940s, it was recognised that care facilities needed to be created outside of the home, and this began with the introduction of childcare centres. The concept of community care saw fostering arrangements made so that looked-after children would be able to remain within a home environment,

DOI: 10.4324/9781003262688-5

and in the 1950s there was a growing focus on the need to try to support older people within their own home environment, rather than them remaining in long-term hospital facilities.

Driven by both financial restraints and the need to individualise care packages, this model triggered the care model that is highly prevalent within the United Kingdom today. In the 1990s a reform of community care was raised on the agenda following the publication of the White Paper "Caring for People" (Griffiths Report, 1988), and local authorities were made responsible for designing community care that provided options to individuals in need of support. This paper emphasised the need to foster independence for the people accessing the services, along with a flexible approach to access of services. However, it also prioritised those in greatest need, and due to financial restraints of local authorities this led to those at the lower level of need unable to access the services put in place, leaving many in a vulnerable position.

Although this paper brought new reform, many areas of the recommendations are still very much the priorities of health and social care today. When New Labour came into power in 1997, they pledged to review social care and the "Caring for People" (Griffiths Report, 1988) reforms were recognised as a challenge to implement fully. Due to this, new grants were introduced which focussed on developing programmes that provided rehabilitation and prevention services and supported those who had not previously met the threshold for accessing care. With a strong emphasis on collaboration across services, The Health Act (1999) saw funding arrangements adapted so that there was one main budget for health and social care, and services would work together in a collaborative approach to individualise care packages to suit the needs of those who accessed support services, with more people being able to access.

This model introduced a different charging arrangement to those using the facilities, as some of the services were free but others required payment for access. Inconsistencies in how local authorities charged led to much discontent and the Government emphasised that they needed to be fully transparent in their work in this area. In 2010, the Dilnot Commission focussed on the cost to families of accessing care support. It identified that half of those over 65 would have to spend £20,000 on care costs, with one in ten faced with costs of over £100,000. The King's Fund (2022) reported that between 2016 and 2020 the request for health and social care support had risen by 120,000 people but that there were 14,000 people less receiving it. The demand for health and social care needs is rising considerably and the United Kingdom is not in a position to offer the services we need, as we live longer and require more support in our older years. The Health Foundation charity (Rocks et al. 2021) estimates that the Government currently has a shortfall of six to fourteen billion pounds a year in this area of responsibility and since the onset of Covid-19 we have seen a huge focus on social care arrangements within the United Kingdom.

With a sector struggling to recruit and provide the facilities needed, now is the time for a deeper analysis of how we can support those who are vulnerable and offer services fit for purpose. The need is unprecedented and organisations such as Age UK (2019) make it very clear that the current model is broken. They report that there are one and a half million people over 65 living without the care and support they need for essential living activities. They call for high-quality care provision to be prioritised, better conditions for care workers and for those providing care within the home to be supported by the Government. We need our Government to look to other countries for alternative models of care and invest in strategies that provide a quality of life, particularly to those who are struggling. Research shows that having co-located childcare and elder-care facilities increases the health and wellbeing of both children and older people and reduces social isolation (Femia et al. 2008). Alongside that, it also reduces the costs, and research from Generations United (Jarrott et al. 2008) in America concluded that those working on co-located sites were able to pool together resources and staff in order to reduce costs whilst offering children and older people a quality service. As educators, we have the ability to take social action and to begin to invest in intergenerational programmes and, by adopting this approach, we are able to support those who may currently find themselves below the threshold for support services. We can reflect on how we can design facilities that welcome our community into our spaces and improve the quality of life for our society. Throughout my experiences of intergenerational practice I have become so much more aware of the benefits and need for this model of learning and care.

Measuring communities' growth

In the eastern Himalayas lies a small country called Bhutan. The country found itself becoming the focus of attention across the globe in 2012 due to its leaders choosing to measure its success through happiness rather than by economic achievement. Frank Martella, Finnish philosopher of wellbeing and psychology, highlighted that traditional measurements of a country's success through GDP (Gross Domestic Product) do not correlate to the wellbeing of a nation (Robson, 2022). Across the globe we are focussed on the economic successes of individuals and societies and this can lead to policy makers prioritising money over the emotional health of our communities. Those who fall outside of working age fall down the agenda and their needs are not valued as important to support. Those of us who have studied child development and researched outcome-based practice understand the importance of building on the holistic skills of individuals in order for them to feel confident and able to lead a happy and successful life. Bhutan's shift in perspective could help us to understand how to reprioritise what is important to us within societies and begin to value those who are not part of economic growth, such as the young and the old.

The United States of America, one of the highest countries in terms of GDP, has seen its economy boom. However, it has also seen the life expectancy of its citizens decrease and inequalities widen. This leads to additional pressures in funding the results of those inequalities and leaves people more vulnerable to negative risk-taking behaviours and less productivity within communities.

Although GDP can measure areas such as living standards, it has the inability to clearly evidence the welfare of a nation's citizens. Our understanding of what contributes to a healthy and happy life needs to be re-evaluated by those in policy-making positions and we need to clearly highlight those who are not represented, in order for their voice and needs to be recognised. The country of Bhutan measures factors such as community vitality, psychological health and cultural resilience and uses the findings of its analysis to build on the country's policies. In 2019, New Zealand Prime Minister Jacinda Arden also saw the benefits of using the happiness index metrics instead of traditional GDP data. Dr. Richard Lango from the London School of Economics said that the New Zealand Prime Minister had set a new precedent, with no other major country explicitly adopting wellbeing as its priority (Robson, 2022). Although, due to the Covid-19 pandemic, these policies have not progressed as effectively as Jacinda Arden had intended, it started conversations across the globe about how to make societies stronger and happier, in turn feeling more satisfied as we contribute to our local economies. These conversations allow all of us across society to begin to deeper evaluate what we need to make our communities happier and more accessible for all within them.

Michael J. Fox (2020), actor and head of the "Michael J. Fox Foundation for Parkinson's Research" flew to Bhutan to gain his own perspective on whether the country was the happiest. Intrigued by the country's commitment to its citizens' positive wellbeing he trekked across Bhutan to explore the impact of using a happiness index and if things were different when a Government focussed on material and spiritual development complementing each other. Bhutan very clearly sees its people's happiness as more important than the material growth of the nation. It was whilst trekking in Bhutan that Michael J. Fox found that his Parkinson's symptoms had improved, and he put this down to being surrounded on a mass scale by the happiness and compassion of people's thoughts and actions. Although there were no scientific explanations as to why his Parkinson's symptoms decreased during his time in Bhutan, there are numerous studies that highlight the impact of positivity, social interaction and happiness on not only our wellbeing but on our health as well. Intergenerational experiences have been shown to encourage more physical movement of older people when playing alongside the children and also improvements to emotional health due to the connections and conversations that come from the time together.

Generations Working Together highlight in their paper "Intergenerational approaches to improving health and wellbeing" (2014) that intergenerational projects build a greater understanding between generations and that through settings engaging in intergenerational practice, they not only work towards tackling social isolation but also contribute to the improved health and wellbeing of individuals. Sir Ken Robinson, an advocate for a shift in our educational models, suggested in his TED talk (Robinson, 2006) that our curriculum systems are still built on an industrial paradigm of education and lead to many talented and creative pupils feeling unvalued and not intelligent. Robinson argues that we need a revolution in education which is rich in diversity and provides a variety of ideas instead of set targets governed by the curriculum content. Intergenerational learning gives us the opportunity to open up new ideas to children and young people, in turn sparking their curiosity and bringing with it an understanding of the purpose of education through the conversations they have with others and hearing their first-hand experiences.

Working collaboratively to build stronger communities

I was fortunate to access support from the outset for our projects by connecting with the Northern Ireland charity Linking Generations (www.linkinggenerationsni.com), the main organisation in Northern Ireland who advocate and develop intergenerational connections. I draw on their work throughout this book as their support and lobbying is highly effective, with a great deal of practical encouragement and research openly offered to support those setting up their own intergenerational programmes and services. This infrastructure enables connections and the ability to share practice, signposting and questions so that groups and individuals can support one another across a diverse mix of disciplines.

As educators, we work within the heart of many communities. Educational institutions are a place where our children grow and prosper. They often sit in an easily accessible position and Governments have invested resources into these areas so that children have the space and opportunity for intellectual, emotional and physical development. Other physical spaces within communities with this level of investment are limited and it is our responsibility to use these as effectively as we can to give children the ability to flourish and prosper, connecting with their surroundings as they progress in our care. These buildings should not be structures that sit apart from the rest of our community, and there is the opportunity to do much more in order for our schools and college buildings to be further integrated into our local societies. With the unfortunate closing of many youth and senior club groups, now more than ever we need to redefine how we use our buildings to connect children with their wider society and utilise the spaces to support those living within it. If we take a lesson from Bhutan, we appreciate the importance of feeling connected and happy within our neighbourhood and we see how this can be effective for supporting the holistic development of children. I am not suggesting that schools should stay open late and offer additional services outside of their usual remit, but instead we should reframe how we plan for our curriculum in order to bring communities together. Throughout this book you will find a wealth of case studies that I hope will provide you with a seed to develop your own intergenerational programmes and I would encourage you to review as a team how your policies and practices can embed intergenerational learning into what you do to open up the experiences offered to your pupils. With this in mind, I will now share how communities have developed spaces to bring communities together at both high infrastructural level and grassroot educational levels.

Redesigning spaces

In a downtown area of Manhattan, New York, a new approach to social housing was introduced with the key priorities to tackle poverty and support community development. Architect David Adjaye designed "Sugar Hill", a social housing complex that represented the community's rich history. The complex provided 124 housing units, alongside neighbourhood facilities such as pre-school education facilities, office units, an art and storytelling museum and a performance space for local artists. David Adjaye designed the complex alongside local people to encompass the heritage of the area and to ensure it was fit for purpose for residents who would be moving into Sugar Hill.

David Adjaye's work on Sugar Hill led to him being appointed (alongside other world-renowned architects) by London Mayor Sadiq Khan to review how the built environment across the city of London could be improved. The architect's remit was to work alongside local councils to create more environmentally sustainable, social and economically inclusive spaces. The approach used in the Sugar Hill development moved away from just providing basic housing but analysed how spaces could be designed to give communities the room to come together and see themselves reflected within the environment. This was something London Mayor Sadiq Khan wanted for the city which he represented. Across the globe we have seen three-generation housing disappear with the changes that have come through economic growth and changing landscapes and this style of design aimed to encourage people to come together more and consider others within their community.

There have been some criticisms of the Sugar Hill complex, with some highlighting that the development did not cater to the needs of older residents, nevertheless it gives us a starting block and an opportunity to review how environments can be designed to facilitate the needs of all residents, whilst supporting the aspirations of our young. The performance and museum spaces that David Adjaye incorporated would be a perfect area for young and old to come together and share creativity and stories. At a community level, we have the ability for social action initiatives that redevelop both our indoor and outdoor spaces within the local community to bring generations together. The arts are a prime example of how this could be done. By creating a local art exhibition or wall mural there is the ability to blend the artistic skills of older and younger community members. Drama programmes could be used to put on performances that share the history of the local community, whilst building the self-esteem and confidence of those involved. There are many types of activities that can be incorporated into community development plans to embed intergenerational spaces into our local areas. Although we, as educators, may not be able to change the built environments of our society, we are able to use these types of projects to review how our own spaces could be used differently to introduce intergenerational learning into our curriculums, enriching the experiences of all involved.

It was on a visit to schools in Madrid that I saw how shared community spaces were used by a range of individuals together. In a city with limited outdoor space, local parks had been reclaimed to suit the needs of those who came to visit. We sat for some time within one of these spaces with the nursery children and it was a joy to see how others would come and go within the park alongside them. Teenage children sat alongside us completing studies together, a group of older gentlemen were working on a woodwork project and talking through their project with the children when they showed their curiosity. There were individuals who took books out of a shared library cupboard to enjoy (with books included for different age groups) and people were working on an allotment space, putting fresh produce to the side for neighbours to help themselves to. The space was beautiful. So well maintained and clearly respected by those who used it. There was no debris, no broken equipment, tools were left untouched in the sheds outside of activity times. The community valued this space and this in turn led to the area being looked after by all residents of different ages. Not only did the children have the opportunity to spend time in an intergenerational space, but they were able to see the values and skills of the adults in their neighbourhood. If the nurseries had their own private playgrounds, there would have been a wealth of missed learning that would have come from spending time in the shared community garden. This type of parallel play is one that can bring many opportunities and connections for children's development.

When we go to parks and recreational areas within the United Kingdom, it is very easy to see the segregation of spaces for different age groups. There are short walks to do where people can have a break and rest on benches. The fields are there for groups to play different organised sports and our young children go to the play park, often placed behind a fence so the children cannot wander out and no one can wander in. How often have you seen people scowling at teenagers when they enter this space, no longer seen as being at an acceptable age to use the equipment? I often ask myself where else do they have to go when I see this. There are ways that we can design our recreational spaces to bring people together, rather than put a further distance between them. We can also implement this within our educational recreational spaces, inviting people in for gardening sessions or walks around the grounds. Consider both your indoor and outdoor spaces and how these can be utilised further.

I have seen one way of how this has been done at our local park. The introduction of "chatty benches" has been incorporated into the design and encourages those who sit there to take some time to talk to whoever they find sat alongside them. There was very limited cost for starting up this project with some benches already in place, only requiring a new sign to be added to them, and the introduction of new ones along the pathways. Through social media and signage, everyone now knows that if you sit on the bench you will find yourself in conversation when someone sits alongside you. The promotion around this was essential for people to realise its purpose and to take time to actively use it. Since the introduction of the chatty benches, a group has been set up to meet once a week at their location and either sit with someone else from the group and chat, or go for a walk together. It shows how one small change can snowball into further progress and bring communities further together. Our individual actions do not need to be grand gestures; we just need to commit to making change and working to our community values in order to bring people together. The park bench has always existed but by rebranding it and highlighting how it can be an integral part of community spaces, we can make a difference. If we can tackle the negative implications of social isolation with at least one person we have already made a difference to society.

Reflection

What these ideas for change show us is that there are ways to utilise the resources we have in order to bring people together. Through collaboration with local councils and policy makers we also have the opportunity to redesign our communities to make them more accessible for all. For those of us working in education, we can review our spaces and curriculum to consider how we can develop these in order to open up the opportunities that we provide to our pupils and engage them with their wider community. We need to stop segregating groups within society and instead reflect on how we can co-design spaces to make them a happier and healthier environment. Age-friendly policies are high on the agenda across the United Kingdom and this provides us with the capacity to highlight the benefits it brings to education. We all have our part to play in making our society somewhere that we all want to live within and feel part of. Through focussing on emotional needs and connections, we also build on the opportunities to learn from others and gain wider perspectives; something so valuable for preparing students for their future lives.

5 Overcoming barriers to intergenerational practice

Schools, colleges and other educational buildings are busy and lively places. Pupils and teachers move between rooms, vehicles are in and out of the car park, parents pop in to see receptionists and teachers. From the moment visitors arrive with you for an intergenerational project, that initial welcome is so important for participants to feel at ease and secure within your school community. Intergenerational practice starts way before visitors arrive at the activity space; your focus needs to be on the relationship built prior to their attendance, their experiences with you whilst there and once they have returned to their daily routine.

Purposeful activities

We have explored the purpose of intergenerational learning and it is important to sit down as a team and with your partner organisations to plan your sessions and ensure that there is a reason for your activities. If you have chosen to complete a project purely for the social experience then that is still a positive experience but be aware that this is not intergenerational learning and should not be recorded as such. For intergenerational learning to work effectively you will need to spend time before the event reflecting on what both groups of attendees will gain from their attendance. Older attendees will not return if it does not bring them satisfaction and your project will soon dissolve if you do not have clear links to children's learning goals. Intergenerational sessions require focus and commitment so make sure to review your intentions prior to the event and reflect throughout the programme on its impact. Through detailed planning, you have the ability to create a sustainable project that will be able to continue to run for a long period of time. Planning purposefully removes the barriers of either group feeling disengaged and ensures that it meets with the objectives of the relevant organisations and settings.

Staff training and understanding

Anything new requires reflection on mindset. For those reading this book, I am making the assumption that you are already curious or engaged in designing

DOI: 10.4324/9781003262688-6

activities that bring communities together. Do not be disheartened if others do not initially show the same levels of energy that you are bringing. With an already heavy schedule, they may be fearful of what additional work the programme may bring or how the programme will fit into the curriculum which they are required to deliver. This is why we need to establish how we plan our activities properly before progressing and reflecting on what learning outcomes we expect to be covered through the programme. It is important to be honest from the outset about how you will approach this: we piloted a project that was not initially linked to curriculum criteria but rather wider topic areas as we wanted to understand how embedding intergenerational practice would evolve. This allowed us to then progress later and map the criteria as we went. This worked effectively with college level students and also allowed students to have more autonomy over their own learning, supporting us in the curriculum planning process, linking their ideas to their learning objectives.

For those working with children and young people, there may be more focus on the activities that take place within the session. Certain areas of the curriculum may be chosen to begin the process, mapping these to the relevant curriculum content. This can be incredibly useful for understanding what particular criteria your programme will cover but also use the reflective sessions and evaluations to review how you can be flexible in your approach and adapt your programme according to the needs of all stakeholders.

When I initially started working in intergenerational practice, I was unable to find any specialised training on offer that I had the ability to access. It took commitment and research to understand how we could design a successful project, and it helped considerably to work with a team who had the skills to adapt and evaluate as we progressed in our sessions. By being proactive in seeking out those who had made a success of sustainable intergenerational projects, I was able to learn from their experiences and gain a much deeper understanding of how things worked in practice. Sometime later, I was very fortunate to be invited onto the pilot of the "Linking Generations" organisation's new training on intergenerational practice. The staff team had worked incredibly hard to design sessions that would benefit those embarking on practice in this area, in turn, sharing their own experiences that generated opportunities to reflect on ways we could enhance what we were currently doing with the Further Education students involved with our projects. This training is now rolled out across Northern Ireland and there are organisations across the United Kingdom and Ireland who offer similar packages. The training gives time to understand the purpose, the practicalities and explore concerns; all essential components for your design and implementation of intergenerational practice. By encouraging all of your staff team to participate in training and making sure that they have time dedicated to attending the sessions allows for staff to gain the expertise from the outset and also highlights the organisation's commitment to making the project a success.

Roles and responsibilities

It is essential to identify the roles and responsibilities of those leading the sessions. You will soon find people becoming despondent in the sessions if they are left to clean up the crafts and snacks resources once everyone has gone or have to organise all the activities independently! Teamwork is essential for a successful project and you will want everyone to feel an ownership of the space in order to create a real essence of community. When introducing intergenerational opportunities I was fortunate to work with a strong and open team who all wanted to embrace experiences that improved our teaching and learning experiences. This sense of trust for one another has allowed us to test out theories and explore our own and students' curiosity, leading to projects such as our intergenerational programme being fully embedded into our course content. It is through valuing each other's ideas, knowledge and expertise that we are able to be critical friends and review in depth what is working well and what may need adapting. That flexibility to our initial vision is important so that we can learn and grow within the programme and meet the needs of all those involved.

Sarah McCully Russell has a wealth of experience in intergenerational projects through her position with the "Linking Generations" organisation. She explains the importance of having a key person with the passion and drive to lead projects and sees this focus as vital for the success of programmes. Although this person brings with them the initial seed of success, Sarah highlights that, for sustainability in the second phase, post-introduction of the programme, it is essential for the full team to take on roles and for the objectives of the project to be mapped into the educational plans and procedures of the setting. Doing this from a strategic level allows the programmes to be integrated officially into job roles and for everyone to appreciate its value. Intergenerational practice requires everyone to understand their role and communicate it. What will you need from policy makers, managers, care home support workers and fellow educators to make your programme a success?

Financial implications

Intergenerational projects do not have to cost a lot of money but there needs to be an awareness of both the costs of the sessions and the hidden costs that could prevent the sessions from running. If you are able to invest some seed funding into your activities, or find some funding from local organisations or councils this can be a beneficial way of breaking down barriers to your events. Your activities may not cost much to run but you may find difficulties in people having the money to travel to your events; those in rural locations may find it very difficult indeed to find ways to get to you.

Although our schools and educational buildings are built to be accessible, the furniture and spaces we use may not be suitable for an older person. You will need to reflect on the environment in which you are planning to host your sessions. Some of your visitors may have physical needs and struggle with the chairs that are usually found within schools. Chairs with strong arms and padded seats are much more suitable for older people's time with you. Talk to the local community groups you are working with and ask if there are any available that you could use or consider if the ones from your staffroom can be moved for the sessions. You want your attendees to have a positive and comfortable time whilst with you and this requirement can hold financial implications on how many people you can have in attendance. Plan this out with your leaders and maintenance team prior to inviting groups to attend. You may find it an easier alternative for your children and young people to travel to the older people than them coming to you in order to overcome this barrier and cost.

Transportation

Our biggest barrier to intergenerational learning activities always came back to transportation. We were very fortunate to have a college bus that we could use to pick up attendees and a very patient driver who was able to support those with limited mobility on and off the vehicle. Few schools and colleges will have this luxury, and social care is seeing increased cuts to their services. One of the biggest cuts we saw was to transportation links and we were unable to bring more people to our sessions, even though we had the space within the building. Partnership working is key here as is finding out what transport your local care homes and organisations have. You may need to adapt your timings for your sessions in order to run your project. Community transport and councils may be able to support you in this area and it can prove beneficial to collaborate with these groups in order to expand your options and ensure you can get everyone to the event who wants to participate.

Timings

We have already started to reflect on timings but it is important to investigate this further before you run your sessions. Our school days are busy, with a huge number of activities to fit into our daily routine. Further complications come when we start to work with care homes and other organisations and find their routine just as busy. Work with partner organisations to find an appropriate time that suits the majority and keep your sessions to a manageable length of time. There may need to be flexibility to how things are run, for example some of our sessions ran over the children's usual break time in order to accommodate everyone. Due to this, within our own intergenerational programmes we offered a snack time to children when they arrived in order to make sure their dietary needs were catered for. We found it a beneficial strategy to start the sessions off with food and beverages for everyone, as this allowed time for building relationships between the generations and put people at ease.

If the sessions are not going to work in your school day, you may wish to suggest a smaller after-school club that brings the community together and is an added learning experience to your curriculum. It is important not to presume that those in social isolation do not have anything planned within their week. We found that on one of the days we were planning to run our sessions it clashed with a local church event, so it was essential we moved our session as most of the older individuals wanted to attend their planned event with the church. By being adaptable, we were able to offer a second event within their calendar and provide further opportunity for social interaction. The length of time for both children and senior attendees is important as you do not want individuals to get bored within the sessions and lose interest. Keep it informal but beneficial for all if you want people to return and continue to participate in your activities. You know your pupils so plan around their interests and learning potential.

Staffing and ratios

Health and social care are under severe pressure. Recruitment is currently a key area of priority for the sector and you may find care homes and organisations unable to participate in your programme as they are not able to dedicate members of staff to accompany the residents to your sessions. We found ourselves in a position whereby some of the groups had to cancel on the day, as they were short-staffed and needed everyone to stay within the care home in order to support the residents. Due to this, we worked with local community leaders to help us to find people who may like to attend our sessions. Talk to your families and to the staff team around you, are there grandparents, family members and neighbours who may benefit from attending? Over the sessions we found this approach a real joy as we got to meet members of the students' and staff's families who we would never have had the opportunity to otherwise. It was an added bonus to find ourselves more connected through this approach and was a very productive way of building relationships with the students that we worked with. Intergenerational practice requires you to step outside your own usual community spaces and it can also help to go and speak to local organisations such as social and educational groups like the "Women's Institute" or "Men's Shed", religious leaders in the community and recreational spaces that run activities for older members of society. Organisations such as "Linking Generations" and "The Beth Johnson Foundation" may also be able to help you with points of contact for finding others that you can be matched with.

When we work in intergenerational spaces, we need to carefully consider our ratio levels in order to ensure that correct supervision and monitoring is taking place throughout the sessions. The skill set of individuals is just as vitally important and we need to reflect on who we need to support us throughout the session. Work within your policies and procedures in advance to review how many staff and volunteers you will need on the day.

Meeting safeguarding and regulatory requirements

Safeguarding can be a problematic area to plan for when leading intergenerational activities. You are bringing a multitude of people together and many older participants will not have been in an educational establishment for a long time. It is not always viable to gain the normal safeguarding checks on attendees that we would have on our volunteers and staff members. This can bring challenges to our usual approaches and require us to look in great detail at our policies and procedures, seeking advice from our local inspectorate teams. Throughout my time working on intergenerational projects (and when working in other areas of practice), I have found that involving those who complete our inspections and the awarding bodies with whom we work from the outset brings a mutual understanding of the benefits of the programme and allows us to develop programmes in a way that satisfies the needs of all involved in education.

Throughout all of our practice, it is essential that children's and young people's welfare is paramount to our approach and that all possible safeguarding measures are taken in order to ensure this. Whenever we bring new people into our setting we must complete appropriate risk assessments in order to ensure all possible measures have been put in place to protect those with whom we work. This may take time to fully iron out but it is an important step in making sure that everyone involved is protected accordingly. Seeking advice from those who have already run projects will help you to make sure that all areas have been covered appropriately. Being aware that there are risk factors involved will help you to reflect on how you design the programme to assure that all parties are cared for with the highest levels of professionalism. Working closely with the parents and families of children will allow for you to explain in detail how you are following appropriate policies and procedures and that children get the very best from the programme.

Health and safety regulations and requirements

Your risk assessments will not only consider the protection of all those involved within the project but also the health and safety requirements that you must undertake before, during and following the time together. It was in my first session of intergenerational practice that I realised just how vital it was for trained care individuals to be in attendance. I had completed my risk assessments, reviewed them with the team accordingly and planned as much as I could. As I walked in to greet a lady she took my elbow and said hello. She then told me her oxygen tank needed to be switched on at a particular time and would I make sure to help her. I felt my heart do a quick flutter before quickly composing myself. I had a quiet word with the care worker in attendance with her and of course, she had it all in hand and told me not to worry. It was a stark reminder of the levels of responsibility that were taking place within the activity morning and a reminder that all of us knowing our roles and responsibilities was key to ensuring all went to plan.

It was not long before it brought me a smile to reflect on how we had brought together so many people with such a range of needs with ease and that even the big concerns such as health support were all covered accordingly so that we could all focus on the main reason why we were there. For our main project we had primary pupils, Further Education students and elderly residents from care homes in attendance. We explained to both the primary and care home management that it was essential for teachers and care workers to stay on site at the college throughout the project and it was a great help to also have their assistants join us to support the development of the programme and help with the play activities that we engaged in. Analysing the care needs and whether the resources are suitable is vitally important in order for your session to progress smoothly.

As educators, we are not trained to deal with the needs of some of our senior attendees and it is important to check in advance that there are adequate staff attending from the community groups to support this area of care. Alongside our groups of senior residents, within our own sessions we also had individuals attend who lived within our local area. We ensured that we contacted them prior to their attendance in order to ensure their needs were met and first aiders were present on site to ensure that if any emergency took place we knew the appropriate person to contact. The individuals who attended independently were aware that they were responsible for themselves and were in attendance as our guests, being given full information in advance on the purpose of the sessions and the expectations we had as an intergenerational community.

When planning for intergenerational spaces, the need to uphold standards we follow within required frameworks and legislation can make it more challenging to meet the demands of paperwork and red tape that come with these. Strong and rigorous requirements ensure that children are protected, whilst in turn raising the professional status of the sector, but there are other approaches that could be embedded at policy maker level to support schools and colleges to integrate intergenerational practice into learning environments. For those of us who hold positions where we can influence change to policies, I would recommend reflecting on how we can do this to provide children with more dynamic and inclusive spaces, where regulations do not hold us back from trying something new that will support our children and young people's development.

Working with parents and carers

Building relationships with parents and carers was essential for testing out a new way of working and embedding intergenerational practice into what we do. Alongside the usual permission letters, we also ensured that we set up information sessions and our values guided these sessions, ensuring an open and honest discussion to explain that we had not participated in this type of teaching before but that we were clear in our methodology. This helped us to shape the programme and to obtain an understanding from families that the sessions would be adapted as we progressed, based on our evaluations and learning. Being honest with your parents and explaining how the sessions will run allows for trust to build and a clearer understanding of what their children will be participating in.

Make sure you explain how your visitors from outside the schools will be alongside trained educators and that the children will not be left alone with any adult visitor or with the young people within the group. If you do not have the ability to host an information session then a video recording that explains the purpose of the project may be beneficial, alongside providing frequent updates during the programme. Asking parents and carers for their input on the value of the project can also be highly beneficial for how you shape future events. An open door, where parents can also partake within the activities can also bring a host of benefits, and we found that throughout our projects by having this open door, we gained great insight from those who we might not normally have the opportunity to talk to in-depth.

Recording the sessions

If you are taking photographs and videos of your sessions, make sure that permission is obtained not just from the children's family but also confirm that you have permission from the senior attendees. Some may not wish to have their images recorded and shared with others so we must respect this as we collate our reflections on the sessions. You may find that some individuals are content for you to use photographs to display within your setting but would prefer for these not to be shared on wider social media channels or websites. Respect their wishes and be sure not to disrupt sessions with needless photos that interrupt the experience of participants.

Past experiences

For some staff and students it can be a challenging experience working with older people due to the care positions they may have found themselves in previously. My own experience in Early Years has found that many of those of us who choose the vocation of care and educational vocations have a natural personality trait of caring for others and this often leaves us taking responsibility for the needs of the family in the generations below and above us. With impairments such as dementia and Alzheimer's disease being a very common factor in later adult life, many of us have our own emotive responses to being within new relationships where this features, due to it triggering memories of how this has impacted our lives in the past with our own loved ones.

I have worked with some individuals where some of the commitments to the project brought with it raw emotion which led to it being too much for them to participate in the sessions. It is important for us to recognise this and accept that not everyone will be in a position to participate. You may find that for these individuals there may be other ways they can support you in the project, through designing resources, invitations or preparing snacks for the group. In a world where we rush, take the time to commit to conversations that reflect on our own feelings and experiences in order to minimise any upset and distress. As your project progresses, individuals may change their mind and may later want to participate. Make time to have these conversations and be led by those who wish to share. For young people, a loss of a grandparent can be their first experience of grief and if this has been in close proximity to the project there may be an immense number of feelings presenting themselves both internally and externally. For some, the experience might bring comfort but for others it could be overwhelming. Responding to the needs of those you work with and gathering the correct signposting to offer them appropriate support is important for approaching the project ethically. The same is to be said for the staff team that you work with. If a staff member has cared for a relative or experienced life being responsible for those illnesses associated with old age, they may wish to step back from the project. Be respectful and mindful as to how you can help and support one another.

The experiences of the senior attendees are also so important to consider. We have found throughout our projects that older people are much more honest and open about their experiences, not always factoring in the censoring of language we tend to put in place within educational lessons. Death, sadness and loss often form a large part of our experiences within later life, and within our own projects we spent time considering how we responded to conversations around this area with the children present. The people who we invite to participate in our sessions are not trained education specialists but instead important pillars of our community who can teach children in an alternative way. This brings a variation to where conversations lead and we made the decision not to give advice on topics of conversation but instead embrace the stories that were shared with us. That brought with it a real boost to our own emotional health, something that we had not expected.

Some of the senior attendees were open about losing their friends, outliving their families and the impact on their wellbeing that ageing had had on them. These were heavy topics but also taught us how they managed this, how they found joy in different ways and why they were proactive in signing up to the project in order to connect with new communities. We have all heard the phrase "things will get better" but this did show our young people that mistakes and hard times do pass by us and we are able to continue on and find happiness. This can sometimes be very difficult to believe when told from our parents' generation but much easier to relate to when we see it first-hand from those who have overcome the many challenges that life brings.

Dealing with illness and grief

Of course, not all older attendees will bring up their experiences of grief, but recognising that death is our final chapter in life, and deteriorating health often factors in the later stages of life, means that working in collaboration with care homes and those with health conditions is an area that will need to be explored and not hidden away.

Throughout our projects, children and young people formed relationships with the older residents from the care homes and there were times when some residents were unable to attend. Children would ask questions around this as they missed their friends and it was important for us to respond in a developmentally appropriate and emotionally responsive way to their questions. In mid-life we sometimes find these conversations much harder. We have experienced loss and we find it difficult sometimes to approach these conversations. Children tend to be much more understanding and it is a good opportunity to teach them how we can show empathy and kindness. Follow up from the session and you might encourage the children to write a letter or create a get-well card for the individual or, if there has "sadly" been a loss to your group, reflect on how the children can celebrate that friendship and show their appreciation of what they gained from them. By having open discussions with the children's family when embarking on the project that you cannot control these human situations, you will be in a much stronger position to deal with any difficult areas that you have to explore.

In my experience, intergenerational practice has actually brought with it mutual understanding and connections that teaches children and young people the value of talking openly and honestly about our feelings. Much of my own practice focusses on the pastoral needs of students and it was heartening to hear students share how they had become much more confident in talking about their emotions due to the intergenerational project. The ability to share how we feel is more important than ever with complex mental health needs impacting on our children and young people. Intergenerational practice gives us a tool for teaching them how to connect and open up with their community.

If a child or adult is struggling it is important for us to signpost them in the appropriate manner. Find out prior to your sessions what agencies and organisations are available to provide support as and when required.

Environment

We have started to reflect on our environment as part of our financial barriers but it is important to evaluate this in further detail as we start to lay out our spaces for intergenerational learning. As we get older, we feel the cold much more and it is important to check for draughts and heating levels in order for everyone to feel comfortable whilst they are with you. Our school environments are built to accommodate large groups of busy people and this can be very disorientating for older attendees who come to visit us. If your spaces are chilly, it is not conducive to learning and people will not engage to the same level.

Walk through your environment from your entrance point. As people arrive, are there steps or difficult spaces to pass over if you have limited mobility? Try not to arrange your sessions to start when there are break times and busy corridors; you want people to be able to have some space to move through and not feel overwhelmed by large crowds meeting them as they enter. This focus from the outset on their arrival will help people to move straight into activities once they arrive at the main space. During our intergenerational projects we ensured to keep parking bays very close to the main space reserved, so that people did not have to struggle through the car park to the main entry point. Throughout our sessions the caretakers were a large contributing factor to the success of the project. They helped us to clear spaces and ensure accessibility, alongside carting much of the resources and furniture for us! Having clear lines of communication to the caretakers prior to the activity sessions made a big difference to the ease of our mornings and they were given information in advance on things such as when corridors would need access, how many tables, chairs and car park spaces were required. It is important to recognise that sessions such as this can add to the workload of already busy individuals within your organisation so that partnership between maintenance and teaching teams was essential and also supported us in completing appropriate risk assessments for the sessions. The sessions actually brought a lot of happiness connecting between different teams and sharing ideas together.

Planning your resources in advance will allow you to focus on the session and prevent you from having to leave the environment to organise different areas. It can be useful to partner with other teachers in your provision for your intergenerational programme as this will not only give you additional support in running the event but it is also a useful way to reflect on how the session has gone and if anything needs to be adapted. Building a sense of trust between you and having clear objectives on what you are going to do will create an ease and bring further clarity on how the sessions will run. It will also allow for further ideas to be generated and more pupils being able to benefit from the programme.

Toileting arrangements

You will need to consider where all attendees are able to use toileting facilities. We cannot expect older attendees to use children's bathrooms, so reflect on the distance between your play space and an accessible toilet for them. This may impact on your ratios when children need to use the facilities as, if children are moving between spaces, someone will need to be with them so you will lose a member of staff from your main session. You also do not want to find yourself in a position where older attendees become lost within your building and unsure where to go, so you may wish to call on the partners you are working with from different organisations to support with directions and moving between spaces.

Collaboration

You will find that collaboration is key to a successful programme, to find out the needs of all residents and to be clear on who is responsible for what task so that people do not feel stressed by the experience. By working in partnership with others, you will be able to match your student groups accordingly and ensure that all parties gain something beneficial from each session. You will be able to start to build relationships prior to the sessions through a range of events and you may wish to set up letter exchanges or video chats between your two groups prior to the time together. This is a great way to build on the relationships between the generations and for you to get to know the workers from the other organisations. Be proactive and open to meeting people who have set up their own intergenerational programmes as, in my experience, I have found many who are very open to collaboration and sharing their wisdom and resources with us.

Communication

Spending some time prior to your programme speaking to your group about how to communicate effectively will support you all in being able to learn through the conversations that take place. This will help the children and young people to develop empathy and understand the importance of thinking of others. Our children are the ones who will lead our future communities so teaching them the necessity of practising values and building strong communities that care for one another will shape how our world will look for the generations to come. During intergenerational projects you may find yourself working with groups with many different physical and psychological needs. We must not ignore this; we must have conversations about how we respond to this in a considerate and ethical way. This is essential if there is a hope of relationships developing between the two generations but fortunately we find children are often able to overcome these barriers much quicker than adults, as they continue to observe and be curious about how others respond. Educational settings can be very loud and echoey spaces that impact negatively on those with sensory impairments.

Frequently those who have intergenerational learning in their provision have had leaders who have been inspired by their learning in this area and then build links with the other intergenerational projects to learn. Sarah suggests using team sessions to review where the team can see links to the curriculum they teach and this in turn leads to planning and implementation being embedded into workloads. Educators are busy. When educational and development plans fully embrace the project, you will find that each person is more likely to fully commit to its success. By using teacher training sessions to review intergenerational learning and see its purpose, you are not asking teachers to go out and find information and add intergenerational programmes as an additional workload. You are committing to giving everyone the skills and knowledge they need to develop a programme fit for purpose. There is a wealth of organisations, such as the Linking Generations organisation, who offer tailored training to review with groups the benefits of intergenerational programmes and provide practical advice on how to make your own programme successful.

When we cannot meet in person

There are many nurseries and schools that have started to embrace intergenerational learning and are aware of its benefits to the children and young people that they work with. The Covid-19 pandemic of 2019 onwards forced us to restrict who we could invite into our places of learning, and this brought many challenges to connecting with our wider community. There were many well-designed programmes that did still manage to bring together our younger and older generations through online mechanisms. However, we are aware as educators of the need to be in spaces without these barriers and the need to engage in meaningful conversations. This is achieved best when we are able to dedicate time to being within the same physical space. However, there were programmes that have continued after the lockdown periods which bring together those who are unable to attend physical sessions. Reflect on this in your designs. There may be projects you wish to run that are held on online platforms and work well for your pupils and the older generations.

We are aware of how digital poverty can lead to further isolation from our society when we find ourselves with it being our main form of communication with others. For those without the skills, resources and ability to connect to the internet there are significant barriers to individuals connecting with technological communities, widening the gap between those feeling engaged with and those feeling isolated from the world. For older pupils, intergenerational programmes that focus on developing Information and Communications Technology (ICT) skills across the generations can be a beneficial way of reducing this gap. Teenagers have lived in a society where technology has been an integral part of their life since birth and there is a lot to be gained from them spending time with older people to grow confidence and share skills.

Flexibility in your approach

Once an intergenerational programme is underway you will see relationships starting to blossom and it is wonderful to observe how much is gained for both young and old from these relationships. This may not come straight away and the patience of all parties is important in this process. You may need to move groups around or increase numbers so that people feel comfortable within the school environment. Reflection will be key to the project's success and it is magical when you do witness the moments of connection.

Learning from global experiences

On a visit to Madrid to visit a number of Early Years settings and colleges, I asked an educator about the inspection process and it was intriguing to hear their response. There was surprise on both sides in our comparison of systems and the way in which the United Kingdom conducted their inspections on educational provision. For them, deep inspections took place within a nursery that had problematic areas, whereas my experience saw all settings inspected on a frequent basis through the appropriate authority. Rather than seeing this as a judgemental process, these were put in place as systems of support to help these settings. The United Kingdom very much views the discourse of childhood through a lens that sees children as vulnerable and in need of protection. I am by no means advocating for the removal of safeguarding policies and procedures. In fact, I feel there is a substantial amount more to do in this area to keep our children across the UK protected, but there are limitations that come from overly prescriptive frameworks and inspections that dull a creative and innovative response to delivering curriculums.

This is why there is a clear need for evidence-based practice to be embedded into our intergenerational programmes and that we evaluate the learning experience that takes place. By doing this, we are able to demonstrate the purpose of what we do clearly and concisely to others who may not attend the sessions. I would encourage you to actively seek advice from those in inspectorial positions such as awarding bodies, curriculum inspectors, registration social services teams and so forth from the outset. Viewing their role as one of support and minimising the fear of their authority, allows for a deeper sharing of expertise and a two-way learning process. In my experience, seeking their support from the beginning of programmes has been a positive experience and created much stronger collaboration across agencies within the sector. We often fear those in inspectorate roles within the UK and we need to rebalance power dynamics within our structures. By working together more closely, we are able to design programmes that meet the requirements and open up new opportunities. All of us want to achieve the same goal: an enriching and positive environment for the children and young people. By having clear lines of communication from the outset of our plans, we can make sure that programmes meet at practice and strategic levels, breaking down the barriers we are faced with when designing a sustainable model.

6 The benefits of intergenerational learning and practice for students

Depending on the focus of your intergenerational activities, the benefits will vary according to the objectives and priorities on which your plans are based. Throughout my experience in intergenerational practice, I have found that there were positive outcomes that I had not expected and this showed me the value of running intergenerational projects with the students with whom I work. All of us gained so much more than we had expected and it became an incredibly satisfying aspect to our learning that we looked forward to. It was from this that we embedded intergenerational learning into our core curriculum and it has kept a diverse collective of students engaged, whilst enhancing their educational experience. The same has been found across age groups and different types of educational settings on a global level.

Students taking the lead

During my first experience of intergenerational practice I was working within a Further Education college. Leading the project were 16–19-year-olds and they were very much involved in the planning, implementation and evaluation of our intergenerational projects. Teachers developed a project-based learning approach to the delivery of our Early Years courses that allowed students to take control of their learning and develop their skills by applying the knowledge of their course curriculum. Project-based learning works across all ages and encourages pupils to develop their communication skills, problem solving, critical thinking and interpersonal development. This collaborative approach to learning encourages us to think creatively and shape how we deliver our curriculums.

Adopting project-based learning with intergenerational experiences at the core is a positive way to provide pupils with real life experiences and gain a greater appreciation for their community. Larmer et al. (2015) discuss the value of this for teachers, as it allows us to move away from the textbooks and turn projects into lessons, in turn not just providing students with knowledge but developing the skills they need as they progress through school and in later life. In a study conducted in Greece, Filippatou and Kaldi (2010) found that primary school pupils with learning disabilities were more motivated when classes

DOI: 10.4324/9781003262688-7

adopted project-based learning instead of more traditional teaching strategies. Pupils also reported that the group work promoted acceptance amongst peers. This is a wonderful approach for ensuring that everyone can feel equal within experiences and gain practical learning that is part of the curriculum which you deliver.

You may wish to adopt a project-based learning approach within your intergenerational programmes in order for you to plan your activities and use the students' progression as part of their evidence towards their specified learning objectives. By taking the lead on projects, students are invested from the start and develop an understanding of the purpose of the activities in which they are involved. Talking with past students who were involved in our pilot project, they recall how beneficial the intergenerational programmes were for their own learning and how it supported them in leadership and management skills which they carried forward into employment. Former student Rachel Pike recalls how special it was to feel as though their work was making a difference and how the creativity embedded in lessons not only brought more confidence when working as part of a team but made the learning experience richer and more exciting.

Emotional health

Initially introduced as a one-year project, the benefits of intergenerational learning were clearly reflected in the students' grades and participation. We could not have hoped for a more effective pilot year. The project saw us working across each generation: children from our local primary school; teenage students; ourselves as teachers in the middle years; and senior citizens from our local care home. The surprise to me as an educator was the students' feedback on their mental health. The intergenerational element of their course had made them feel more connected to the college, their community and the wider organisations of the social care and Early Years sector. The relationships built with the senior attendees were discussed with love and gratitude. The appreciation of senior members from our society actively listening to them and sharing their experiences made a great impact on the young people and allowed them to consider different topics from a new perspective. Student Leah Johnston told us that experiencing intergenerational programmes within the college would be something that she would carry forward into her vocation as an Early Years Educator. Leah feels incredibly proud of working towards tackling social isolation within her community and found that the project boosted her confidence and self-esteem as she knew she was able to lead a team in the planning for the intergenerational events. This experience is not one that we would have been able to provide without the intergenerational experience in which Leah was involved. Research commissioned by Linking Generations (2021) report "Education and intergenerational practice" found that intergenerational experiences not only had educational benefits but also supported children and young people in feeling more connected and understood within their societies.

In a research project undertaken in America (Park, 2015) with eight- and nine-year-old children they found that the approach created better psychological outcomes with a decrease in anxiety and an increase in self-worth.

All of us working across education are aware of the vital need to prioritise children and young people's emotional wellbeing. The increase in the number of children and young people with depression and anxiety is becoming a devastating normality across society and must be seen as a key area of work across all disciplines. Children and young people need to develop the skills needed to look after their emotional health just as much as their physical health and, by creating spaces for generations to come together, you are in a position to encourage all participants to build on their psychological skills through the art of conversation and sharing of experiences. If we reflect back to Chapter 1 and the frameworks provided by Maslow and the Blackfoot community we know that we need to feel part of a community and have our emotional needs met in order to prosper and reach our full potential.

Supporting families

As educators, we understand the importance of building secure attachments for children in order for them to have the confidence to flourish and prosper whilst within our care. We work with families on a continual basis, to support them in raising content and hopeful individuals who will have the capacity to grow into successful and happy adults. Within our society, the traditional extended family is something fewer of us experience surrounding our child and adulthood. This can leave parents with fewer opportunities to observe parenting practices and to gain confidence in their ability as parents. This lack of support can leave parents struggling to equip themselves to deal with the challenges that raising a child can bring. Living in a world where we now have a tendency to blame individuals for not achieving desired outcomes in life, how much better would it be if in our societies we created more environments where support and care is offered for one another in a nurturing and non-judgemental manner? For anyone reading as a parent, I am sure all of us can relate to the harsh judgement that can come from strangers if our parenting style does not conform to their expectations.

Intergenerational programmes widen our support network and provide us with an opportunity to learn from those who have experienced many of life's ups and downs. If parents are encouraged to get involved with your projects it brings conversations with an older peer who may be able to pass on their reassurance and kindness, whilst also giving supportive tips that encourage us. When my own children were born, it was a welcomed comfort to have my mother come to stay for a week and support me as I got used to the new routine. Her listening and gentle advice gave me that confidence to know I was doing okay. Not all of us have this luxury of an extra pair of hands and very often our older generation are afar. The relationships that blossom during intergenerational programmes can help to build on the influences in the child's and parents' lives in a positive way and give them all someone else who is there to listen.

Developing positive secondary attachments

Our secondary attachments (those that come after our relationship with our mother) in childhood are vitally important, particularly in the early years as children start to learn how to build relationships and self-regulate their emotions. You may wish to rethink how you design parenting programmes by embedding an intergenerational learning experience into its structure. When designing parenting skills programmes to support the primary and secondary attachments that children have, these must be planned for in a way that empowers the individuals and does not leave them feeling insecure in their role as a caregiver. Intergenerational sessions are a beneficial way of supporting parents in their confidence as it allows time with others who have experienced the trials and tribulations of family life.

In 2007, John Bowlby's son Richard Bowlby continued his father's research on theories of attachment and discussed the importance of the secondary attachment figures in a child's life. He concluded that children would feel more secure and confident in life when they know there are other people, away from their parents, who will put their needs before their own. In strong, extended families both the child and the parents can gain support from these secondary attachment bonds. Those without these support mechanisms may find themselves isolated from their society and without individuals who can step in and help when it is needed. We need to do better as a society to prevent these families from feeling this isolation and reflect on how each generation can be brought together to support one another and blend generations together so that love, knowledge and care can be shared and we can create our own "extended family" within society. Different generations have a range of factors that may lead to them feeling isolated from the wider world, but this loneliness leaves us with the same feeling of disconnection and sadness. By building connections between different age groups we have the ability to feel more secure and attached to our surroundings and more confident in a variety of skills. This mutual benefit is what will make your projects strong and give everyone a reason to want to participate.

For those of us without extended families, long-term intergenerational programmes allow relationships to develop and support to be given not just to the younger and older attendees but also to the parents in the middle generation. By building support for, and the confidence of, parents we are able to build better outcomes for children through the development of parenting skills and confidence in their own role within their child's life. Throughout our projects, we found parents much more likely to attend our intergenerational programmes than other events that we hosted and on review of feedback it was the informal atmosphere and the mutual respect that came from spending time amongst different generations. Our children and young people will develop closer relationships through their secondary attachments as through your role modelling they will be able to see the strong support network that surrounds them.

Students leading change

The snowball effect from our intergenerational project was an absolute pleasure to be a part of. Local councils had committed to "age-friendly" practices and saw this grassroots project as a way to connect with a diverse range of ages and visited us frequently to interview attendees and support them in their planning for progress in our community. Students' confidence grew and they presented their findings to local teachers and principals. We returned to the attendees of these events some months later and found that all had gone on to implement their own intergenerational projects within their own schools. Our open-door policy for the project led to local educators requesting to attend the sessions and they were able to understand how it worked in practice and then implement the same into their own settings. It was wonderful to see local playgroups and nurseries running their own intergenerational activities in a way that suited their children and families. The project had gone from a small class-based activity to becoming a linchpin for a best-practice model for implementing intergenerational learning. For students to see that their work was inspiring others (and often those with a great deal more experience and qualifications) was a turning point and they were able to appreciate that they could make positive change.

Within two academic years of our first project starting, it had been successful in reaching the Finalists Stage of the Association of Colleges Beacon Awards for the most innovative practice for social action and student engagement across the United Kingdom. The process of the awards allowed students to gain a further awareness of how vitally important their work had been and saw them commit a fresh energy to what was important to them as individuals in relation to their society and values. Our model design had not been implemented to gain awards; it had been put in place to offer students the very best opportunities to develop their creative thinking and learning, whilst taking social responsibility. However, the Award gave them (and others) a pedestal to try something new in the classroom and for us as teachers to be brave in how we approached our planning and delivery for lessons. Every session was underpinned by values and we were able to evidence the strength of this through outcomes for students and their commitment to their course programme and curriculum.

Moving forward, the teaching team have remained in contact with the first students who participated in the project and we have been able to see how this has supported them in their practice and been embedded into the Early Years settings in which they now work. It has been a pleasure to see how the ripple effect of one project has continued to be adapted in order to suit different educational settings and wider community organisations. The most important aspect of our planning was that students were leading the experience. Not us as teachers, not policies, not indicators. The students' roles were to seek the purpose of the activities and take ownership of their own learning. By planning around communities, we were able to see vast improvements in student engagement and participation. This in turn led to institutional adoption of this type of approach and increased collaboration with other colleges. The experiences in which students were able to participate were much broader than our traditional approach to teaching and learning. This sharing of practice allowed for educators to develop their teaching skills further and in turn provide students with an even better educational experience.

Developing connections further

This approach to our practice brought new relationships and a deeper connection to our local community. Not all of us were raised locally (myself included) and we found ourselves gaining a better understanding and connection to our local spaces. Students had to step up during these exchanges, there was no hiding behind others as all of us had a clear role to play within the session and we saw students trying things that they may not have done in the past. Celebrating and appreciating this helped to secure our own relationships with students and gave them the courage to recognise how the small wins are much, much greater than they may initially appear.

When the Covid-19 pandemic hit and we were forced to move to online classes, one of the first questions students asked was how we would continue to connect with the people we had worked with during our intergenerational project. They were immensely aware of the social isolation of many of the attendees and recognised that the requirements of staying at home would impact this even further. The project had not only supported students in their learning but built their confidence in taking social action and analysing together as a team what they could do when faced with barriers. Within a week, schools and care homes were connected by the students through letter writing, and a plan was put together for an online art project. Both were led by the students, not by the teachers, and as I walked through my own town later that week, it brought me happiness to see the artwork collected by the students pinned up on the windows of one of our local care homes. In the most difficult of times, students had managed to keep us together.

Believing in our students and providing a space where they have autonomy to lead the plans for the classroom is a truly wonderful experience and allowed me to see how students commit to reaching higher educational outcomes, whilst also realising that their voice is important and can bring better things for themselves and others. Pupils at all ages have the most exciting and creative ideas for connecting people together and work effectively when you encourage them to show you how we can make those changes as a team. Trust in them and you will see everyone flourish and commit to making society a better place for all generations. Student Leah Gervin shared with me how the intergenerational projects had extended her college experience and given her time with older people, something she would not have had normally. Leah valued how the project had given her more confidence and she had gained a deeper understanding of other topics that were not part of her Early Years course such as Health and Social Care and Social Policy. Education allows us to plant the seed of curiosity in pupils and provide a space for them to explore which path they want their future to take.

Increasing understanding across generations

A report by The Economic and Social Research Institute published in 2021 stated that young people in Ireland would be financially worse off than their parents (Roantree et al. 2021). Rising housing costs and salaries plateauing have led to this being the first generation since records began to have lower living standards than the previous generation. Alongside this, the report identified that young people had been disproportionately impacted by the Covid-19 pandemic. During this time, the rates of unemployment in this age group had been the most seriously affected. These findings were not exclusive to Ireland. The Economic and Social Research Institute (ESRI) (2021) highlighted similar concerns within the "Closing the Gap" report. They highlighted that the younger generation did not spend as much as the previous generation on non-essential items and this was due to factors such as low wages, high debt and fewer working hours available.

The ESRI report identified that the United States of America and the United Kingdom were already finding themselves in this position. In Western society young people are educated more than any generation before them; however, they have also had less subsidy from local authorities and their parents than previous generations would have gained. Although those with a degree are not earning much less than previous generations, student debt is rising and those who have not progressed to Higher Education are now earning over 50 per cent less than they would expect at this stage in life. As it stands, our youngest adults have had to live through two recessions, they see a world uncared for and their world has been hit by the climate change crisis, alongside the fear that has come from growing up with numerous global terrorism incidents. There is a lot of pain and hurt for this generation when they realise that their life outcomes could be more unfortunate than those who came before them. In many cases, this leaves some bitter feelings towards older members of the community who did not have to face these challenges.

Intergenerational experiences allow us to develop our understanding of one another and prevent bitterness across the age groups. We need more understanding in the current climate and to build communities where we appreciate the value of one another. Through conversations and time together, there is the opportunity to understand that the opportunities may have changed but we still hold similar values and have all had to face different struggles as we progress through life. The same can be applied to how older people view youth within their community, and through the projects you are able to establish new and important relationships where people can explore common ground and look at ways in which society can be more accessible and happier for everyone within them.

Our future leaders

In the UK, we are currently facing a health and social care crisis and the Government has made clear that the cost of caring for older people is not covered by current budgets. Not only are the prospects bleak for young people in many respects but the financial burden of funding care facilities will have to come out of *their* tax once they reach the employment stage of life. All of these worries continue to further build resentment and division across generations. The current health and social care crisis should be viewed as an area of concern for all of us, both now and in the future. We need to realise that the current model (reviewed previously in Chapter 4) needs a re-design and young people will play a part in carrying forward plans that are put in place over the next decade to establish this.

Intergenerational programmes allow students to see the benefits for all age groups sharing spaces and connecting in a variety of ways. During one of our intergenerational programmes we were able to see children and older people creating plans to make our community spaces more accessible for all and gaining a mutual understanding of what the needs of each group were. In a society where we often no longer live within "three-generation homes", we need to break down the walls that separate us and get to know one another more deeply, so that we can develop empathy and care amongst one another. In doing so, we are showing our children and young people that there is hope for their future and that the investments put into developing more effective care services is important and relevant.

Case study: Connections over technology

During the lockdown of 2020, we lost the ability to run some of our intergenerational programmes and it took us time to refocus on ways in which we could still connect the children and senior members of our college community. Running letter exchanges was a beneficial way of keeping momentum (discussed previously in Chapter 2) and bringing hope, as we all had to isolate. However, as we moved forward into a world that saw some spaces opening up widely and spaces such as our care homes still very much at risk, we needed to look at alternative approaches. This transition was key to us; a way of building relationships prior to a time when we could come back together in the same physical spaces.

I asked Sarah McCully Russell from Linking Generations how she had seen other organisations do this successfully and it was through this conversation that we put together our reading programme. This programme saw Further Education students allocate time each week to read to older residents of care homes, followed up by some social conversation exchanges. We recognised that this was not directly linked to the learning outcomes of students' curriculum but instead brought different benefits that would support students in their practice, confidence and literacy skills. For many of us, public speaking is a task associated with anxiety and there have been many occasions in my role as a Lecturer where I have seen students grimace at the thought of standing up in front of their peers to present.

This programme, where students would have to read a book publicly on a social media platform, was viewed differently by the students to traditional styles of presenting. Working with Early Years students, having the ability to be storytellers, singers and engage in conversation are essential skills to develop for the job role and this was the perfect way to encourage students to have fun with storytelling and feel at ease sharing their voice with others. As students progressed through the programme, there was no pressure for anyone to read if they did not want to but we saw students wanting to participate, as they recognised the value of the task.

Books were chosen jointly by students and senior members and it brought time for us to be present and relax into the space where we were. We knew our focus was getting back to a position, after the lockdown period, where we would be able to invite young children and senior adults back to the college to meet physically but this reading programme brought much more than we had anticipated.

The value of connection was so important to all of us following such a lengthy period of time where care homes had been completely isolated from visitors, and it gave us a lot of happiness to receive feedback on what it had brought to the care home residents. In a conversation with another educator running a similar project, they told me that a resident from a care home had told them how grateful they were for the project as they had thought during lockdown that they would never have the opportunity again to have a conversation with a child or young person. The scale of how important connection is really is evident in feedback such as this. The reading project was a brilliant way for teenage students to engage with their community and share and build on their skill set. Their feedback showed that they really enjoyed taking the lead and we saw it raise their confidence in other areas.

This type of project can work extremely effectively when working with students studying English and Literacy modules, by spending time focussing on particular texts and sharing it with others for discussion. There are many opportunities where an "intergenerational book club" could be run, to shift from intergenerational care to learning. Spend some time reflecting on how literature could be used in this way within your setting and how online mechanisms can connect us. The time to explore literature and texts together, with a wealth of people with different ideas and viewpoints can be a wonderful way to enrich the student experience and build further on their knowledge.

7 The benefits of intergenerational practice for communities

We have explored a range of benefits to intergenerational practice for learning and emotional development but there are many other ways in which your work within this area will impact positively on your local community and wider society. Throughout each project that I have been part of I have used evaluations and networking to review the impact of the embedding intergenerational learning with individuals and wider groups. This has allowed a deeper appreciation and understanding of what ripples of change have come from the connections. The great philosopher Confucius said: "If your plan is for one year, plant rice. If your plan is for ten years, plant trees. If your plan is for one hundred years, educate children." Your intergenerational projects will teach children the skills to take care of those around them, highly valuable attributes and qualities needed for our future leaders who will have the ability to make positive change and build a more vibrant and exciting society. Mutual respect across generations is also incredibly important in order to tackle discrimination and prevent divisions between people within a community. Through these relationships, we are able to learn from one another and experience a wealth of knowledge and expertise being shared with us. This role modelling and mutual sharing of skills can only bring more to our communities and make places happier and open for all. Within this chapter we will explore further the different benefits that bringing an intergenerational project into education can have on the wider society.

Social isolation and loneliness

Social isolation and loneliness are classed as separate concepts but the fluidity between the two is important to be aware of and understand. Social isolation can happen when we find ourselves with limited friends and relatives to surround ourselves with, whereas loneliness can leave us feeling vulnerable and disconnected due to a lack of social relationships with others. Many may find themselves in a position of being socially isolated but still feel content in their surroundings and be happy to find themselves with only their own company. There are individuals who do this through choice and prefer to live an isolated life. The problems occur when that choice is not ours to make and as we get

DOI: 10.4324/9781003262688-8

older, many find that their friends and family have passed on, moved further away or we are not in a position to travel to other areas as easily as we once did.

Our health, economic and psychological position can impact this further and lead to additional isolation from our communities. As an educator, I know how it feels to return to work after the summer after having a period of time off. There are unsettled nerves: will I still know how to do my job? Will I get on with the new people I meet? What will be expected of me this year? If I now imagine myself at home with limited people around me, my legs struggling to walk a distance and worrying whether I have enough money for the travel fare, my awareness of the psychological implications of returning to social events would be far more intense.

Our health status can contribute to our feelings of loneliness and isolation. Poor physical health prevents us from being as active as we once were, limited mobility makes it difficult to travel far and sensory impairments can make busy places feel overwhelming. As we get older, illnesses such as dementia can become a feature within our lives. In the United Kingdom it is estimated that there will be over one million people living with dementia, and this number is rising due to our ageing population (NHS, 2020). Symptoms of dementia such as memory loss, confusion and problems with speech will lead to further risk of isolation as people feel less able to live a full and active life.

The World Health Organization (WHO) is focussing deeply on tackling social isolation, and intergenerational practice is a very beneficial approach to tackling ageism within societies. In 2020 the WHO launched their plan for "A Decade of Healthy Ageing" that calls for Governments across the globe to rethink how we think, feel and act towards ageing. Advocating for age-friendly environments, intergenerational spaces will be an important factor for bringing different generations together and making society friendlier for those marginalised to access and feel part of. Wales has seen their Government implement the "Well-being of Future Generations Act" (Welsh Government, 2015) that makes it a legal responsibility for public bodies to consider the long-term impact of decisions they make and to adopt a collaborative approach across stakeholders in order to prevent consistent problems across the Welsh societies. Wales have been the first to implement such an Act and it has attracted much interest from across the globe as it puts the onus on policy makers to make a positive and long-lasting change, not only for the current generations but also for the generations to come. Those leading the way are showing great awareness of the power of intergenerational services and education and how mutual respect across generations makes life better not just for now but also embeds sustainable models of practice for the future.

Isolated communities

By implementing intergenerational projects, our experience taught us that we had the ability to reduce the social, geographical and emotional isolation in our local area. Working within a predominantly rural location, this was incredibly important as we find many of our local senior citizens do not have neighbours nearby and have limited social groups close to their homes. By 2028 the older population within rural locations is set to rise by 149 per cent across the United Kingdom (Commission for Rural Communities, 2012) and there is a need to review how we as a society will ensure that those living in rural locations will not become isolated from their wider community as they enter into older life. There are physical health risks to social isolation as well as the influence on our psychological health; Holt-Lunstad et al. (2015) found that factors such as social isolation influence our mortality risk just as much as other risk factors, such as being a smoker. There is an incredibly important need to reflect on how we can ensure all people in both rural and urban areas gain connections and social experiences to prevent them from living within an isolated neighbourhood.

With decreases on spending across different areas, it is time to think creatively as to how services can collaborate to minimise costs. If you are working within a school or college within a rural area you are in a prime position to provide a space to bring people together in order to tackle social isolation and it will not only benefit your pupils but also the wider community. In Chapter 6 we explored barriers to intergenerational working and for many of us in more urban areas we need to highlight to local councils and policy makers the importance of community transport links, wherever we are able. Talk to these individuals, present the case as to how it will not only meet with your educational objectives but also with wider outcomes, in turn minimising the need to create new spaces for people to come together.

Discrimination

Both young people and older members of our society experience age discrimination. I am sure if we were all honest enough, we could admit that we have found ourselves making pre-judgements of others before we get to know them. The World Health Organization (2021) has challenged Governments to recognise that ageism is a global problem which leads to poorer health, social isolation, earlier death and costs economies billions of pounds. For younger members of our society the WHO reported that ageism is associated with poorer physical and mental health and that, around the world, an estimated 6.3 million cases of depression are linked to ageism across the age groups.

Vicki Titterington from Linking Generations worked on a project with police and community safety officers and found the project supported young and old to begin to understand the value each brought to society and to break down the stigmas that were held towards each age group. This led to further projects being implemented across Northern Ireland and has now found intergenerational practice becoming a key element to building communities and tackling ageism. I am sure all of us appreciate that we need to do more to stand up to discrimination. By embedding intergenerational programmes into your settings, you can create a mutually respectful environment for people to gain a deeper understanding and appreciation for one another.

Increasing life expectancy

Our grandparents are living longer. We are all living longer. Retirement now brings with it the opportunity to embrace a whole world of possibilities and it is important for us to recognise that when working across generations. We will be working with a wealth of capabilities and potential. We have heard the expression that "50 is the new 40" and this continues way beyond these years. Retirement now gives us the time to learn new skills, travel and volunteer in a number of roles, in order to do something rewarding and for a purpose that we feel is important to us. If we think back to Chapter 1 and the Blackfoot community framework we can consider how skills and knowledge can be passed down within society in order for people to feel they are part of an important network and can carry forward expertise that may have been otherwise lost. Early Years pioneer Maria Montessori said: "Feeling one's own value, being appreciated and loved by others, feeling useful and capable of production are all factors of enormous value for the human soul." As a society, we must start moving away from devaluing people once they retire and not recognising the valuable contributions that they still make. Intergenerational programmes can lead to you finding a wealth of expertise that can bring education to life, whilst in turn providing a platform for older people to share their passions and past experiences.

Improving digital skills and minimising digital poverty

The rise in digital tools has allowed us to connect in new ways and this has provided a link for children to maintain relationships with their wider family through platforms such as video chats, messaging and social media sharing. With this rise of new communication techniques, we see digital poverty impacting those without the skills and resources to access these. An important element of intergenerational learning is to ensure that all ages are able to use the technology we have, in order to stay connected. The Centre for Ageing Better (2021) report that around five million people over the age of 55 are not online, which impacts on their social communication and activities such as booking a doctor's appointment, accessing bank records and finding support services.

When we reviewed the grassroot projects globally within Chapter 3 we saw how educational settings had set up their own intergenerational projects to bring older and younger people together to share learning whilst helping one another with practical tasks. Older pupils supporting those senior to them to learn how to complete activities such as shopping, booking appointments and researching online can provide older people with skills that will enhance their lives and, in turn, offer the opportunity for an array of discussions that can support younger people in learning about budgeting, planning and a wide range of life skills.

Digital case studies: Shifting to suit the climate

During the first lockdown of 2020, many of us did not believe that technology would be able to connect us across communities. Throughout that year we moved rapidly: I saw so many creative ideas across different types of organisations that managed to develop programmes that were truly inspiring. I remember my friend's father getting in touch, someone who had never needed to use technology for planning, asking me to show him how to design activities for a Scout Group "away" day. Usually there would be over one hundred young people getting together to camp and engage with the elements through playful activities but this was not achievable with the restrictions. Through connecting across generations, he learnt how to design an action-packed day with quizzes, tournaments and fun activities to teach children about the world around them in order to build their confidence and understanding. It was a delight to hear, after the event, how he had used his time to learn and that it had resulted in such a wonderful day for the young people, who had so very little to entertain themselves with whilst they had had to stay at home. In retirement, he had committed to lifelong learning and engaging the Scouts with their Leaders in a way very far removed from how things usually worked for the groups. Without intergenerational exchanges he admits it was highly unlikely the event would have gone ahead.

We saw this across organisations and community groups and it was so interesting talking with Lynne Bennett from the Linking Generations organisation about her experiences of an online project during the lockdown period that had come from a meeting with a school. In one of my roles I am Governor at a local primary school. As a report of the school's activities took place one evening, my ears pricked up when I heard intergenerational practice being discussed. It was of great interest to me as I had been delighted when I saw the head teacher at one of our own college events earlier in the year, where students had organised a seminar to discuss the benefits of intergenerational practice to educators, and I was even happier when I had seen projects spring up following this. It was a great boost to the students to see that their experiences and presentations had influenced change and inspired others who worked in leadership roles within the sector.

The school had done marvellously with implementing intergenerational learning opportunities but, like many of us, it was challenged as to how this could run without us all being physically present within the same space. After months of Governors' meetings that had a very deep focus on Covid-19 policies, procedures and decisions, it was wonderful for me to hear that projects were starting back up, particularly when intergenerational work formed part of it! I listened to the discussion around the project and it was really good for me to understand how the project had run from the other side, rather than me being involved with the planning and delivery of the sessions. It was evident that it had been a success and had brought great delight to the teachers and children, but what was most interesting was that this had been an online programme rather than the two generations being together in the one building.

Children had engaged with many different creative activities such as "pots of kindness", planting seeds and decorating pots that would go to the care homes, along with painting rocks with bright cheery pictures and adding kind messages and quotes to their artwork. Within the care home, activity coordinators supported residents to partake in similar activities appropriate to the residents. For some attendees within the care home, they felt at ease listening in, conversing and observing without the creative element. The final products from the creative rock painting sessions were then added to the care home gardens. Whilst the children engaged with their creativity, they "Zoom-called" the residents and Lynne Bennett helped lead the two groups in conversation with a range of prompts. For Lynne, it was a game-changer: she had not felt prior to the event that online projects would work effectively, but it was during this programme that she realised how much benefit it brought and how useful it had been for connecting those residents with limited mobility and with a variety of needs.

The residents involved would have found it very difficult to leave the home under any circumstances, regardless of Covid-19 restrictions, and may also have found it very tiring having visitors in with them for a prolonged period of time. This unexpected situation that we all found ourselves in inspired new ways of working. The project shows how moving away from a one-off event where pupils do something kind for local older people can be developed into a long-term programme that really engages all within its activities. The teachers could have very easily spent some time with their children making cards and gifts for the local care homes but they went one step further and sought out how they could focus on building relationships outside of the school and get the most from the project. It shifted from being an act of kindness to an intergenerational learning opportunity and children engaged throughout with the conversations, using the video-calling system with residents of the care home, whilst engaging with the fun side of the project.

This project was testament to how online platforms can bring a different approach to our planning for intergenerational practice and it is one that will continue within the school and in Lynne's roll-out to other educational settings. We have explored barriers in detail within Chapter 6, but this is one project that has shown that approaching barriers with a solution-focus allows us to design strong and sustainable projects that bring a wealth of happiness and learning for all those involved. Children felt more connected to their community in a time of isolation and older people were able to observe the care from others, whilst learning and fun took place.

Reminiscence

During one of our intergenerational sessions, I had a conversation with an elderly gentleman. We had music on in the background and he shared stories of his times in dance halls and the fun he had had during his youth at these. He told us that it had been a long time since he had last danced and a colleague asked if he would like to dance with her. He did and it brought such happiness to see him enjoying something again that he had not been able to do in a long time. My colleague asked him why he did not go dancing any more, and the conversation that came brought some sadness. He was very honest and explained to us that he was at an age where most of his friends were gone, he had outlived many of them. We realised that he had not come from part of a care home group but instead had visited us independently after he had heard about the sessions. He continued to talk and explained that the last time he had been out was at our last session, the month before.

During our reflection time after the morning's activities, we found ourselves being drawn back to this conversation. It had been a brave step for the gentleman to come and see us on his own but it also highlighted the need for more opportunities for our neighbours who lived independently to come together. The space brought time for people to have conversations, enjoy something different in their life and move outside of the four walls of their home closing in on them. There was a large scope of learning objectives that had been set for that session that day but what had become the most important moment of the session was for us as a group to recognise just how isolated some people are and the importance of social time incorporated into spaces. Social time gave us an opportunity to laugh, smile and reminisce together, sharing experiences and stories that were important to us. Our cultures are built through the sharing of stories and we need to make sure we find a balance within our life to make time to sit and listen. Both sharing and listening to one another brings a great deal of benefits to our emotional health and wellbeing.

Reflections: The value of play

Throughout my children's primary years, they spent a lot of time with their granny whilst my husband and I were at work. During the summer months when I would be off work, Granny would tell me how much she missed the routine of collecting the children and spending time with them, so we would work out some time for them to still spend together. For her, it gave her a sense of purpose. She had her own routine and commitments so we were careful not to overstep the free childcare, but, having days where Granny brought out the fancy biscuits and listened to their woes from their school days built a strong connection that will stay with the children throughout their lives.

I noticed when I collected them the importance of not rushing off halfway through a quiz show, it was an integral part of their time together and they would share knowledge together to beat the participants on the television. They worked diligently together as a team, sharing new and old experiences such as a popular band's song title, a history answer learnt from school, a piece of knowledge collected by Granny over the years. Play is a way of connecting us together and an essential part of life at any age. Within intergenerational learning we can adapt play to suit the different generations and play such as quizzes and table-top games are a great way to draw people together to share.

Our first intergenerational programme began with a game of bingo and it was an instant hit. Others who had run projects often mention to me the success of bingo as a game to incorporate. In fact, as I write I remember both sides asking as they came in if we had a game of it planned for the session, as it was so enjoyable!

There are two elements to this story that show the benefits of intergenerational practice to communities. The first is the ability for myself and my husband to be able to be economically active thanks to the support structures of our own parents providing a happy, safe and stimulating environment to our children. *The Scotsman* (Bradley, 2020) reported that around 14 million grandparents in the United Kingdom provide regular childcare, saving families £22.5 billion in childcare expenses. I appreciate, that for some, this arrangement is not always the preferred option by either party, but during my experience the benefits it brought to all of us was huge. As we live longer, more active lives, the opportunity to be hands-on with our grandchildren is a huge benefit in a field of areas.

The second element as to why this story was important to share was that it highlighted the benefits of play. Whether we are at home or in our organisations, play has a deep impact on our happiness and learning. Games such as quizzes and bingo are ones that all generations can connect with and share knowledge. The laughter and fun in turn brings the opportunity to relax and engage together. With mental health of all ages currently a major concern, we know that connection, laughter and a chance to switch off from our own stresses are all vital components for dealing with anxiety and worry. It is much easier to start up conversations when we engage with play and connect with others, building relationships within our programmes.

Increasing fathers' participation

By creating spaces where we bring our older society into our educational settings, we in turn have the opportunity to bring parents into our provision as well. Parenting programmes often see a higher intake of mothers' involvement and we are aware of the positive impact an engaged father will have on a child's later life outcomes (McAlister and Burgess, 2012). High levels of fathers' involvement are associated with better physical and mental health in children, higher educational achievements and lower substance abuse. However, many parenting programmes do not address the role of the father in parenting, and intergenerational programmes can give us the opportunity to design sessions that support fathers in their confidence in parenting and provide a space for them to understand more about their child's learning and development.

Throughout our own intergenerational programmes, we found fathers were more responsive to attending alongside grandparents than with programmes designed specifically for parents. They took a practical role in providing transport to older attendees and then found an interest in the hands-on activities that were taking place within the sessions. It led to us shaping our provision so that we could run sessions that fathers could feel part of as well as our older attendees and we have since led workshops that incorporate Men's Shed (2021), a charity set up to provide spaces for men to "connect, converse and create", to help us collaborate with local organisations that support men's emotional health and also provide an opportunity for men to teach children their skills and feel valued for their knowledge that they can pass onto others.

We also had many attendees join us from local rural locations and focussed on our garden space to reflect on how we could use this area to engage with our fathers and grandfathers, offering them the opportunity to share with the children their agricultural skills and knowledge. The use of outdoor spaces allowed us to learn and connect together in a beneficial and productive way. The adults sharing their knowledge taught the children about the seasons and produce; the ways to build allotment vegetable beds; and making different woodwork resources, such as bird boxes. The practical activities gave us time to converse and share learning and experiences together, whilst also providing information to fathers of the benefits of play opportunities to children's development. This helped to build the fathers' confidence in seeing their value in spending focussed time with their children. By making our programmes inclusive to all generations, we are able to engage a much wider intersection of our community and build on children's sense of belonging to their local area.

Diverse childhoods

Within one of our programmes, the school that we were working with had recently admitted new pupils who spoke English as a second language. Students planning the sessions were encouraged to reflect on how we could support all children in their language and communication skills and used an intergenerational space for this. Using play-based learning, older and younger people explored their experiences of their local community during childhood. For each two children we had one senior person in attendance and as they sat around tables in larger groups they compared their experiences of their local community and how it is used. This resulted in wider discussions of experiences of childhood across different countries, and older attendees reflected with the planning team after the session how they had found the experience really useful to challenge some negative perceptions that they may have previously had of people moving into the local community. By the end of the session, the young children had taught them new words and greetings and new friendships had been struck between young and old. The time had been so beneficial not just for its initial purpose of focus and language development, but also for the wider discussions that had taken place. The bond continued each time the sessions ran and it's evidenced how we can challenge negative perceptions in a safe and proactive way where everyone can show their true selves and find mutual understanding.

Kierna Corr, from a nursery school in Northern Ireland, shared with me a story from one of the sessions that was held with a local care home. The community is made up of diverse backgrounds and within her pupil group there was a new child who had come to them from Portugal. The child had a limited extended family unit in close proximity and seemed to enjoy the opportunity to meet with older people. In one of their earlier sessions, a Portuguese resident of the care home noticed the child and began to sing songs in their native language. As Kierna recalls the moment between them, it clearly brought deep happiness to both of them. The child was in awe, totally lost in the rhythm of the songs and amazed that someone knew the songs that had been shared from birth with them. The elderly man found a tear escaping from his eye, a joyful tear of connection.

Health benefits from intergenerational relationships

There was a key moment for me when I realised just how important and valuable this project was. I was told, prior to the arrival of a group of older adults, that one of the attendees had narcolepsy and her care worker asked me to be aware of this as activities took place. It was a defining moment when, at the end of this session, the same care worker came to talk to me again and encouraged me to look at the table where the lady was sat. It had been an hour-and-a-half session and the care worker told me that back in the residential home the individual fell asleep every ten minutes or so. This was not something that had come through ageing but something that the individual had lived with all their life. At this point in the session, where we were drawing to a close, the care worker had been observing intently throughout the morning's activities. She was overwhelmed that this was the first time she had seen the lady not drift off and was delighted with the interaction she was having with the children alongside her at the table. After spending a period of years within the care home, a thriving and busy centre full of activities and interactions, it was overwhelming to find that one morning with the children had kept her so alert and focussed on the tasks in hand.

It made a huge impact on me, as an educator, to see what small interactions can do in relation to our health. It was a joyous moment and one shared with the rest of the staff team at the residential home once they went back to their usual routine. I have no medical evidence for the reason for her staying awake but those that worked with her everyday were adamant it was from the connections that came that day. When I asked her if she had enjoyed the morning, the response was beautiful. She was not aware that she had not drifted off but she was aware of how much she had enjoyed the time spent with the group of children. For that one moment alone the project was a personal and professional achievement. We had made a profound impact on at least one individual. This was the first of many moments of happiness and, in turn, led me to realise the true importance of intergenerational experiences for the children, for us as teachers and for the older members of our community.

8 How to make intergenerational practice work in education

Regardless of the age of pupil we work with, there are many activities and programmes we can implement in order to enhance the curriculums which we deliver. Nurseries, schools and colleges have used a number of approaches to support intergenerational practice and seen how this enhances learning, as well as the social benefits that they have brought. Throughout this chapter we will explore the different types of activities you could plan as part of your programme and explain how it can link with the curriculums you follow. View this as a starting point and adapt these ideas to suit the individuals you are working with, alongside their interests and experiences. By doing this you will be able to hold the engagement of the participants and utilise the skills of the older people who attend your sessions. Throughout our own planning experiences it has brought great benefit to involve the students in discussions of how the intergenerational learning experience will look as it develops a sense of ownership and commitment to the project. The same applies to staff teams, and encouraging them to share their creativity and innovative ideas as to how they feel sessions will benefit their various topic areas of learning. Even if you work in one area of education, please do read through the rest as it may spark an idea as to how it could be adapted for the age group that you work with.

Intergenerational learning in Early Years settings

Peatlands Playgroup in Northern Ireland shared with me their simple plan that they presented to parent and carers at the start of the year, alongside a meeting with them all to explain the benefits and practicalities of intergenerational sessions. You will see from this plan that it is very loose but it gives them a theme for their monthly visit that relates to the general areas of learning that the children would be engaging with at that time. Playgroup Leader Estelle Brownlee explains that having an overall plan allowed for flexibility and also for impromptu activities to be introduced following the children's and older participants lead. The team considered how the activities could promote children's holistic development, whilst also holding the attention of all of those involved. The setting follows the Northern Ireland Pre-School Curriculum and has taken into account the different areas of learning set out in this curriculum and tried to incorporate a range throughout the academic year.

Although the plan is simple, you can see how it would promote engagement for both children and older participants through active learning and give space for conversations, play and collaboration. Consider what celebrations you usually have within your setting and how you can shift this from performances to intergenerational exchanges of learning.

This type of plan could work for any age group and provide you with the scope to create a rota among teachers to lead a session each month, decreasing the workload and not leaving it to fall on one person's shoulders. You may wish to consider the events you host throughout the year and reflect on how you could extend these further in order to incorporate social intergenerational learning activities.

Table 8.1 Pre-School curriculum plans for intergenerational activities

This year's events:	
Date:	Activity:
November	**Picture bingo, fun and games.** *Supporting mathematical & intellectual development through play, whilst building on our relationship with our new friends.*
December	**Christmas sing-along.** *Scientists in Sweden have found singing together in a group is just as beneficial as physical exercise for our health. A Christmas carol is hard to beat as well!*
January	**Stories both old and new.** *Children will make their own stories in playgroup to bring along to this and then get the chance to hear a range of stories from our friends.*
February	**What makes us special – Valentine fun.** *Whilst enjoying Arts and Crafts we will focus this session on what is important to us and why respecting differences is good for everyone.*
March	**Music and movement.** *This session will focus on our physical movements and exploring different instruments. Children will make these themselves and our friends will be able to share their musical skills!*
April	**Easter bonnets and bunny crafts.** *Children will be able to decorate their bonnets using a variety of materials and making some great designs. Through the Easter story we can look at the importance of caring for others.*
May	**Helping hands – potting plants.** *Children will decorate their pots using hand painting before learning about different plants, how they grow and how we look after them.*
June	**Summer tea party.** *Celebrating the end of the year's events, we will spend our last session with a special party, some treats and an array of traditional games.*

Intergenerational learning in primary schools

To support children's literacy, a primary school in County Tyrone, Northern Ireland, approached parents and carers to ask if the children's grandparents would be interested in signing up to a reading exchange called "Reading Buddies". The grandparents would attend on a weekly basis and support children in paired reading. It provided the opportunity for one-to-one support for children, in order to improve their reading ability and also developed strong connections for children and senior members of the community. The school's head teacher reported that this was a constructive way of gaining extra support for the children who would find it beneficial to participate in one-to-one time in order to enhance their vocabulary and literacy skills. In turn, the head teacher received positive feedback from the adult attendees who supported the programme, as they felt valued for the help they were offering the children and enjoyed exchanging stories with them.

With schools limited in time and resources to offer one-to-one programmes, this brought the opportunity to provide more support than the school would usually be able to do and although they had run similar programmes like this within the school with parents, it had sometimes been difficult to find volunteers due to parents' working commitments. The older participants had more free time available to offer the necessary support and were also able to learn new skills through the school's online library system that the children showed them and they loved learning more about the children with whom they were buddied, through the conversations that took place. By offering time for initial chats at the start of the session and focussed discussions on what they had read together during the session, intergenerational learning took place on both sides and strong relationships between the pairs developed. It was also a positive way for the school team to get to know families better as they began to spend time with some of the children's grandparents who volunteered on the programme.

From this the school have now incorporated intergenerational activities into their curriculum plans and their outdoor area has been developed further through the conversations they have had with older people who came along to help with the reading buddy programme. A local women's group now comes in to teach the children how to care for the flower beds and vegetable patches, donating flowers to brighten up the space. Another community group has built sheds for them and taught the children woodwork and design skills appropriate to their stage of development. The difference in the space has been dramatic and really enhanced the learning environment, with children now spending much more time outdoors learning than they would have previously.

I am sure all of us have been in a position lately where, due to limited funding, we have had to reconsider programmes that we run and making links with the local community to directly support areas such as literacy can be a very useful way of gaining that additional help to which a child may not currently have access. We are aware that the longer a child goes without intervention in relation to reading, the wider the gap will be as they grow older. In the Literacy Trust's "Read on, Get on Strategy" (Douglas et al. 2016), they reported that the reading gap between boys and girls is one of the widest in the developed world and if we do not get our children reading, it will cost the economy £32.1 billion by 2025. This is a serious problem that we need to deal with immediately and not allow children to fall through the gap, moving through education without the basic literacy skills required in later life. By encouraging grandparents to get involved with projects, you are providing a space for role modelling and showing the grandparents their importance and contribution to the children's learning. If it is not possible to gain a family group for support, you are still widening the support network around the child, and the informal approach to an older friend sharing reading time with them might remove the pressure on the child to *perform* and instead gain an appreciation of the fun side of reading.

Intergenerational learning in secondary schools

A secondary school head teacher from County Fermanagh, Northern Ireland outlined their intergenerational learning programme to me and explained how it had been built around developing three core areas: English, Maths and ICT. Through a project on sustainability and how to tackle climate change, the pupils worked with older people to consider how they would do this within their own community. Teachers were asked in advance if they would like to be part of the project and this allowed for a review of how the three core areas could be embedded and extended alongside these.

The project started by participants reviewing the outdoor space and developing a sustainable vegetable patch together, before moving on to the next topic of food wastage and preparing a recipe book on how to make meals from leftovers and store cupboard provisions. Maths skills were developed through budgeting and reviewing ingredient costings, and pupils were also able to develop their creative media skills through the resources that they designed and created.

As the sessions progressed, some reminiscence sessions were included into the history classes and pupils were able to hear about what their village used to be like and how the older participants would "make do and mend", linking into the sustainability topic. Throughout all the sessions the pupils recorded their learning and experiences using technology and taught the older participants how to use the different apps and equipment, providing a mutual learning space between the two parties. Pupils' feedback included that they found it much easier to write their English and History essays as they had a better understanding of the topic through hearing it first-hand.

Here we can see how a school has considered how certain subject areas will benefit from the incorporation of intergenerational learning and how to build a mutually beneficial space. Through using innovative ideas they have been able to make the curriculum come to life and used the knowledge of the older people to teach the children in a more informal way within their school. Reflect with the team as to who would be interested in engaging with intergenerational experiences and use a training day to come up with projects together that can lead to more team teaching and student-led sessions. It is important to review how plans can be blended together but team teaching provides pupils with more attention and develops a cross-disciplinary approach to learning where educators are able to learn from one another and share responsibility. In Ireland, team teaching is integrated into educational policies and is a key area of learning within initial teacher training (Rickard and Walsh, 2019). It is considered integral to promoting inclusion and integration. For newly qualified members of staff, it can be isolating going into a classroom on your own, and team teaching is a highly effective way of providing an open space to discuss teaching and learning. It also challenges those who have been in the role for a longer period of time to try something new and be open to trying something different. Adding intergenerational projects can be a dynamic and exciting way to encourage educators to work together more.

Intergenerational learning in colleges

Further Education colleges have an abundance of spaces for a variety of vocational areas. This puts them in a strong position to be leaders in intergenerational practice. Further Education was where I gained my first experience of intergenerational learning, through the development of a project-based learning approach as to how the delivery of our Early Years courses would be run with students. We designed an informal café to bring together a group of young children and residents from the local residential homes and our local community. When we first designed it, we were unsure of the response we would receive from our local community. We were aware that there were risks to leading learning using this method; however, the benefits outweighed these greatly and we were excited about trying something new, innovative and values-led.

The Early Years students used their initiative to meet up with different professionals to develop their concept of the intergenerational café and plan for each session in detail. Working with Early Years or Health and Social Care students would be the obvious area for learning around this practice; however, we were able to soon see how it could support other curriculum areas within the college. Our hospitality students were highly involved from the outset by planning and serving snacks and beverages, meeting the dietary needs and requirements of our young and older attendees. (It must be recorded here that the feedback on the quality of the hospitality students' fruit scones always featured highly in our evaluations!) It was wonderful to collaborate with a different group of students and for them to also make the connections with the attendees whilst the hospitality students were able to work towards their practical assessments during each of the sessions.

Intergenerational practice can support many vocational areas. There are our trainee hairdressers who can get the opportunity to develop intergenerational connections whilst developing their skills in working with clients and hairdressing experience. Sports departments are able to design activities such as chair exercises and low-level aerobics that suit older individual needs. This may be an area that can be harder to find during their work placement experience and so brings an opportunity for them to analyse how participation changes when younger children are also in attendance. Media students can support with marketing information of the event, writing up case studies and supporting the front-facing team with evaluations. Horticulture students have many practical activities that they need to undertake. Intergenerational practice allows them to evaluate outdoor spaces, creating and designing environments and activities that can support sensory experiences.

Those studying joinery are able to lead workshops on making different resources and teaching young children new skills whilst also possibly getting the opportunity to learn skills from those who have worked in those roles before. For the Early Years students it was a requirement of their framework to undertake literacy and numeracy courses alongside their main qualification. Through this project they were able to see the value of both these areas. In order to run each session, the students had to work within a budget, plan ratios, collect data for their research and, through these tasks, we were able to build on our mathematical skills and link it to an area of learning that many of them had previously found challenging. Our communications, newsletters and worksheets for children, as well as our speech, had to be appropriate, clear and professional due to the spectrum of organisations with whom our resources were shared. Alongside this method of developing literacy and language skills, there was also the wealth of stories and conversations in which we participated and upon which we reflected, that supported students with their confidence in public speaking and questioning.

Particularly as we were trying something new, it was important for us to have an open learning environment where people were able to visit and explore the benefits of intergenerational practice. Throughout the programmes we had an abundance of visitors, both internally from our Higher Education (HE) courses and externally from local and international HE students who were undertaking research in this area. They were able to interview staff, students and attendees to explore what intergenerational learning brought to each of these groups, and this fed into a wide scope of research projects. We asked in return for their openness in sharing their findings with us, in order for us to learn more and better understand the impact of our work.

It was not only the students with whom we worked that conducted research, but also the staff team who were enrolled in a number of professional development courses. At the time I was undertaking my own Master's degree and chose to focus my research on literacy learning for young children and the impact of intergenerational experiences on this area of development. A colleague was undertaking her Early Childhood degree and also found that intergenerational programme was an area on which she wanted to focus in order to complete her dissertation. Her focus was on children's social and emotional development and both my own and her enquiries led to us further developing and strengthening the programme by reflecting on our findings and sharing this with both the course teams and with the students. It was a valuable experience for students to share in their teachers' learning and to be part of that process. They would frequently ask about progress and what we were learning and we hope that we provided them with the opportunity to see themselves studying for the same qualifications in the future and to role model to them the importance of being lifelong learners.

Intergenerational learning in education

Throughout all these projects you will have seen how educators have built on what the children are already doing in order to enhance pupils' learning, rather than applying intergenerational learning as an additional piece of work. It has also shown us the importance of finding local settings within the Health, Social Care and wider community network who want to engage and on whom you can rely for support. Throughout my experiences in intergenerational learning I have found that these networks help to build open and honest spaces where people help one another and provide feedback on how you can improve your spaces in order to connect with older people.

Each of the settings has reviewed their curriculum and considered the needs of their pupils, reflecting creatively on a different approach to traditional teaching strategies. This approach requires trust and flexibility from the management team and it is important to communicate with leaders as to what your expectations are for the project and how it will meet with all of your settings policies and procedures. There may be some nervousness and apprehension about embarking on something new, but if you have planned in detail and shown where it links and improves student experience and learning, then the risk you take will pay off with the showcasing of the students' efforts.

9 Adopting a multidisciplinary approach to intergenerational practice

When I started working on intergenerational projects, I soon found a wealth of expertise from local professionals and organisations that were there to support us throughout our experiences. There is a great deal of knowledge and research that has already been gained in this area of practice and I would encourage you to reach out and talk to these individuals before commencing on your journey into intergenerational practice. There is no reason to reinvent the wheel but instead draw on the research and practice that is out there and adapt it to suit the individuals with whom you work. When I first embarked on my journey on intergenerational practice I was surprised and pleased to find many people locally who were only too willing to help me with setting up a project.

Throughout this book I have spoken about the organisation "Linking Generations" as they really have been integral to not only the team I work with, but a huge number of projects across Northern Ireland and internationally. I meet with Vicki Titterington who is the Director of "LGNI" to discuss the work of the organisation and their adoption of multidisciplinary approaches to intergenerational practice. Vicki is a lead expert in intergenerational work and has spoken at conferences across Europe, America and South Korea to share with others the organisation's journey to support others to embark on their own intergenerational projects.

Providing infrastructures for intergenerational practice

Meeting with Vicki from Linking Generations, I learn that the organisation was founded in 2008 and Vicki has been with Linking Generations from the beginning. Initially working on setting up six intergenerational projects across the country, the small team began working with schools to discuss the benefits of intergenerational practice. As the organisation developed, they found themselves in a position where others were being signposted to the team for advice and guidance on setting up their own intergenerational projects, so the move was made to put together a business case to turn Linking Generations into a sustainable organisation that would focus on four key areas: linking projects; providing tailored training; distributing small grants; and advocacy of intergenerational practice. There was some initial concern in relation to moving from practice to

DOI: 10.4324/9781003262688-10

providing an infrastructure, but the transition led to Linking Generations being the key organisation for support in this area of practice throughout the whole of Northern Ireland.

As the team began reaching out to schools, they realised that there was a lack of research and evidence to back up the reasoning behind this approach and they identified that not only did intergenerational activities support emotional wellbeing and social time together, but they also benefited educational outcomes for pupils. The need to showcase these benefits led to the organisation focussing on research on intergenerational activities that they could then share across multidisciplinary stakeholders. There has now been a variety of research projects completed and these are accessible on Linking Generations website (www.linkinggenerationsni.com).

Vicki shares with me the organisation's ethos of working collaboratively and explains that having these resources online allows others to access evidence to support their own projects when applying for funding or designing their own programmes. For those of us developing our intergenerational practice, this ability to use their research freely is of vast benefit to access support for our own institutions. Not only does it allow us to back up our approach and adopt evidence-based practice within intergenerational programmes but it gives us the ability to learn from those who have invested time and resources into this area. You will find similar resources and research papers from The Beth Johnson Foundation (www.bjf.org.uk) and the organisation Generations Working Together (www.generationsworkingtogether.org).

The organic and responsive approach adopted by Linking Generations has led to 11 network groups set up across Northern Ireland and the team also participates in multidisciplinary groups where often the main parties are from statutory agencies. This representation allows others to understand how intergenerational connections can bring positive outcomes across an amplitude of disciplines. Linking Generations guidance also shows individuals how to set up collaborative projects across services to bring communities together. Vicki explains that this approach makes you feel like you are part of something bigger and builds the confidence to embark on intergenerational practice. The team's determination to connect and communicate with grassroot projects brings them the ability to link people together so that you can find others completing similar projects to what you intend to do.

The diverse group of individuals that sit within the local networks brings its own set of challenges for Linking Generations as they can range from local volunteers who support projects within their community to large organisations that support specific areas. We all bring with us a great array of agendas, and Linking Generations work effectively to identify how these can all be met in an effective manner collaboratively. The strength of the presence of such a range of disciplines means that there is representation at all levels from practice to policy, and Vicki has seen statutory bodies paying much closer attention to the benefits that intergenerational experiences can bring across educational and community development plans. By raising the profile and advocating the need for generations to come together, Linking Generations work has led to all council areas embedding "age-friendly" plans across Northern Ireland and including intergenerational practice within their strategy; the organisation's research has helped to inform community plans for the better.

The ripple effect across disciplines and organisations is key for Vicki and she explains that the team make it clear from the outset that when you embark on the training and adoption of intergenerational practice the organisation will ask you to return to them following your experience to share its effectiveness and the benefits it brought. They work tirelessly to support individuals and organisations and in return, when you meet with them again you are encouraged to share this so that others can learn and be inspired to try out their own intergenerational activities. By telling others about your journey through social media, videos, articles and case studies, the team can see how this leads to others gaining the knowledge and confidence to begin their own journeys within their institutions. The small grants and training support offered by Linking Generations is seen as a catalyst to something bigger and Vicki takes great joy in seeing how a small seed has an impact not only within settings but also across communities.

Vicki shares a recent example from working with a professional from the War Memorial organisation who set up an intergenerational project and then shared his experiences with the Ulster Museums. His story being listened to online led to all of the museums' outreach workers training with Linking Generations and embarking on their own intergenerational projects. Vicki understands that communities are much more likely to listen to links they are sent than from organisations sending over literature and this is why she values this circle of communication throughout others' intergenerational projects. Vicki explains that the implementation and evaluation stage is vital for them, as this is where they are able to identify the benefits and understand how projects have worked in practice. When individuals share their stories, and by Linking Generations sharing the research undertaken, others are able to see that intergenerational programmes are not an add-on to what is already being done but instead a redesign of existing mechanisms for learning and connections to make what we do more effective.

In the autumn of 2021, care home staff were under immense pressure following the lockdown periods and the continued need to protect those vulnerable individuals within our society. Vicki found it heartening that many care home activity coordinators requested training with Linking Generations to see how they could successfully implement their own intergenerational programmes. Vicki puts this down to the organisation having the strength of research behind them and also due to their "Care Home Friends" who have worked with Linking Generations in the past and now take the time to share with others how beneficial it has been for their setting and the residents with whom they work.

There are always concerns within the voluntary and charitable sector that funding may cease and Vicki is realistic that the organisation needs to be flexible and responsive to need, in order to continue to be sustainable. She adopts a positive outlook to this, however, and explains to me that if Linking Generations were to cease in the next year, their legacy would continue through the work of those who have connected with them. Multidisciplinary working has led to changes across the Province to make intergenerational learning an established practice across settings. She is aware that intergenerational practice would probably disappear from policy agendas without the representation of Linking Generations in multidisciplinary groups but, at grassroots level, the work would continue and she is rightfully proud of the impact the organisation has had on education and communities across Northern Ireland. By working collaboratively across disciplines, Vicki considers how the discussions lead to others recognising that intergenerational is not just something *nice* that we do within organisations but instead something vitally needed within our communities to tackle a spectrum of areas from health to isolation.

Multidisciplinary thinking in education

One of our key supporters for our intergenerational projects was the local council, who were incredibly supportive of our events and helped us to highlight the work we were doing. By working collaboratively with the council we were able to blend community and educational outcomes together in order to give students a much richer and more stimulating experience during their time with us. Students saw themselves as part of the community and were able to have their voice heard, speaking at council events and gaining an appreciation that what they were doing was having a direct, positive outcome on their community.

When we work in multidisciplinary teams, we build on our own knowledge and skill set, developing areas of practice that we may not have had experience in before. By working across disciplines, we increase our professional status as we access continuing professional development opportunities that may not have been accessible prior to these partnerships. Working in more inclusive ways and opening our doors to others offers us the opportunity to review things from another point of view and develop programmes that enrich children and young people's lives and supports their holistic development.

There is no denying that funding options for new projects are limited across education and community development. Collaborative working allows us to pool our resources in order to be cost-effective and provide those within our societies a better experience. You may find it challenging at times to understand the different perspectives and agendas from those from different disciplines but listening and removing our egos from our practice supports us in our understanding and allows us to develop programmes that support a range of outcomes for those in attendance. Working in partnership with other disciplines enables us to understand the services and professionals who work within our local areas, and this can provide valuable knowledge on where to signpost individuals and at the same time build a dialogue between organisations to promote joined-up thinking and a community approach to planning and delivery.

As we have reviewed in previous chapters, the segregation of groups of people leaves large sections of our society isolated and disconnected from our community. We appreciate that we need to do more to bring people together and we can begin that journey by bringing together our services and working in more collaborative ways. Multidisciplinary working is not new and a statutory requirement was incorporated into the Children Act 1989 (Legislation.gov.uk, 2017) for those professionals working with Children and Young People to work better together in order to protect them and give them better life opportunities. Agencies such as Sure Start, the Youth Justice team, Children Services Planning, and the police now adopt collaborative approaches to connect services and provide our communities with stronger networks of encouragement. We still have a long way to go and, as educators, we still need to gain a deeper appreciation of what can be gained from working across disciplines. Education can be a lonely place when we step into our classrooms and it is not just outside our organisation where we can learn new disciplines, but also from our colleagues. Seek out the change makers and encourage the adoption of sharing practice within the organisation to learn and grow alongside one another. In Matthew Syed's book *Rebel Ideas* (2022) he reminds us to look outside of the echo chamber that we often find ourselves in so that we can diversify our thinking and discusses how, by bringing together bigger groups of alternative perspectives, our own bias can be challenged, leading to greater growth and innovative ways of working. We know that older and younger people are often marginalised and it is important for us to work with others to break down this stigma in order to create more prosperous societies.

Reflect on who you can work with to diversify your services and bring new energy into your educational provision. Our young and older people have many similar needs and I have learnt a great deal from Health and Social Care Professionals that can be adopted into my teaching practice. Consider who you will open up thinking spaces with to grow intergenerational practice both within and outside of your organisation.

10 Planning for intergenerational practice

This chapter will provide you with the principles needed to design your own programmes within your educational setting. It will be important for you to consider those you work with and also the individuals with whom you are partnering. There is not a "one-size-fits-all" approach to intergenerational learning, and what may work for one group may need to be adapted to suit another. During our own intergenerational programmes we partnered with different senior groups. Some were more active and physically able than others, so different activities were run depending on what worked for participants. The same principles can be adopted but your plans will vary depending on who you are working with and what your outcomes for the project are.

For many educational settings, the importance of projects linking with direct areas of the curriculum will be a key aspect to planning. For others, there may be consideration given to children and young people's social and emotional development and a different style of project is identified. In order for your projects to be an on-going feature within your setting you will need your plans to be fluid and adaptable. Ensure that they are regularly reviewed and amended when needed. Listen to those who attend and participate, taking the time to sit alongside others and consider what they have to say. For us to build communities, we all have to feel part of them and have our voices heard. Although we explore evaluations in Chapter 12, your evaluative processes need to be considered from the outset to ensure that this is not an afterthought but something that allows you to adapt and refocus throughout each session. Use this chapter alongside the templates to put together your plans for your projects.

Risk assessments

The preparation of risk assessments can be problematic when working with such diverse age groups and needs. It is vitally important to be honest and open with the partnerships you are working with and ask for clarity and information as your project progresses. My experience of running intergenerational learning projects has found that you cannot always anticipate what is going to be said or what is going to be needed. Talk to your parents and carers in advance so that they are aware of the activities and ensure that they agree to all aspects of your plans. We have discussed the health and safety and child protection requirements throughout this book but now is the time to investigate closely how your policies and procedures will be met throughout your intergenerational project. Reflect on all aspects of the session, from people arriving to the follow-up of the programme.

Template for risk assessment

Your setting will have their own risk assessments that are important to use to ensure you are meeting with the policies and procedures but here is an example form that could help you to ensure you are minimising hazards and risks to the session.

Table 10.1 Risk assessment template

Project name:

Dates of project activity:

Timings of sessions:

Location:

Signature and name of lead individual responsible for overview of risk assessment:

What are the risks/hazards?	Who is at risk?	Control measures:	Risk rating (1–5)	Preventative measures:	Action by whom and when?	Completed:

Finding participants to attend the sessions

In our modern technological age, we find ourselves used to communicating via emails and a variety of social media channels. When we first started working on intergenerational projects, we quickly learnt that this style of communication was not conducive to finding individuals and groups to work with. We had to get out into the community. We visited the care homes and explained what we were doing and met with local leaders of community organisations to explain what we were trying to establish. We had to build the relationships before the project commenced in order to build trust and understanding, and we were questioned intently by our senior guests about the purpose of our project.

They were interested but we had to acknowledge that they had a very clear routine and had enough experience in life to not sign up to things that did not engage or stimulate them. Our intentions and plans had to be well thought out and explained in a clear and informative way. We also had to ensure that it was a fun and happy experience for everyone and make that clear in our explanation to individuals. If you want your project to be successful, there must be investment into the relationships you want to build. Put together plans of when you are able to go out and meet with people and talk them through each aspect of your sessions and build your project on trust from the outset. If you can take some of your pupils to explain it, that would be even better. We will review evaluations later in this book but make sure you incorporate time for feedback on each session in your plans and review how this can be embedded into the following session. Feedback should be gained from all attendees in order to fully appreciate the experience of all those involved, allow for you to build a sustainable partnership with all service users and make intergenerational learning a core aspect of your delivery within the setting.

Sensory impairments

Your sessions may include people who have a diverse range of sensory impairments and you will need to consider in advance how the layout of your environment and the activities you prepare take this into account. Small groups within your main classes will help to support conversations and minimise embarrassment of people having to ask others to repeat themselves if they cannot hear. Your resources are also important to review and you must ensure you do not expect everyone to be able to do what you can. Older people may struggle with holding pens or participating in craft activities so consider how you will adapt your activities to ensure that everyone can be involved throughout the session. You may want to encourage the children to record ideas and annotate conversations to build on their literacy and writing skills. If you have tasks that will be completed during the session use both verbal and non-verbal instructions by explaining what will happen during the day but also having a pictorial and written explanation for individuals to review and return to. Work with those who know the older group and establish the needs of the individuals and how you can support them.

Introductions

I always find it strange when we take children to an event where they do not know anyone and tell them to "Go and make friends". We do not reflect on our own responses to being within a new group and I for one would be reluctant to walk into a party and interrupt someone in order to introduce myself. Even if you have completed activities to get to know one another prior to your first face-to-face session, encourage everyone to introduce themselves on arrival. You may wish to design name badges as one of the first activities so that people can see these throughout the session and know what name everyone likes to go by. Other "get to know one another" activities could include sharing our favourite things to do, best reads, a story of something important to us. This helps to develop relationships and embed a values-led approach into the space.

Introduction activities

Table 10.2 Table of "Introduction Activities"

What values are important to us and why? Encourage the group to reflect on what is important to them and let the pupils record a design that could be displayed on their table.	**What do we have in common?** Set a task for the attendees to think about the spaces they share, their families, the places they have been etc. to find out more about one another and find common interests.
Words and phrases that we use. Have a list of different groups such as: children, older people, greetings, emotions etc. and ask the group to explore the slang words that they use across the generations.	**Design a community flag.** If our town/village had a flag what would it have in its design to represent everyone within it? Ask participants to design their own flag that incorporates the diversity of the group.

Physical spaces

When we first started our own intergenerational projects, it was important for us to consider the physical needs of our attendees. The initial group of senior citizens we worked with had mobility requirements and so it was our responsibility to assess the best matched group of children for them to work with. We chose to run the sessions with a class of seven- to eight-year-olds as we felt this age group would benefit from the play-based opportunities but were also able to do this through table-top learning and find it easier to sit for the session than a younger child may. If you are working with younger children you may wish to use a larger space so that there is a bigger area for activities to take place and to minimise the risk of younger children knocking into the adults. We discussed in detail spaces within Chapter 5, and I would suggest returning to this section when reviewing your physical space.

Behaviour

All healthy relationships start with respect for one another, and an intergenerational project may be a very different experience to that which children and young people have experienced before. There will be a variety of needs from both parties and it is important to set the boundaries prior to your sessions so that everything runs smoothly. As discussed when reviewing physical spaces, when we first started with intergenerational work we were working with senior adults with mobility and sensory needs and it was difficult logistically to bring very young children into the provision we had due to their tendency to be more interactive and physical in the younger years. We planned an array of play-based activities so that we could ensure that attendees would not get bored and would fully engage throughout the session. For those of us without mobility or particular sensory needs, it can be very difficult to relate to how overwhelming busy spaces can be and therefore we must ensure that we speak to our children and young people in advance to explain to them how vitally important it is not to rush around or move away from the areas that we have asked them to be within.

Children are very observant and responsive to the needs of others and may often recognise these before we do. By explaining to children, in advance, in an age- and developmentally appropriate way, that older participants may find some things difficult or complicated you will soon see the children's awareness and a mutual trust being built between the two groups. In discussions with other educators, many have found that children who are often louder and more excitable within their usual classroom are able to focus and are more relaxed within an intergenerational space. It is really important to establish boundaries with participants and to reiterate throughout the session the need to listen to one another and not talk over others. Having additional people from the Education and Health and Social Care teams will help you to manage the session effectively and create a calm atmosphere for everybody to feel relaxed within. Intergenerational practice is very much about respecting and caring for one another's needs so it is up to you to consider in the planning stage how you will make the environment comfortable for both the children and older people.

Example of boundaries to include for your sessions

Table 10.3 Example of boundaries to include for your sessions

Expectations for the session:
• Be kind. • Consider others. • Listen to what others have to say. • Tell someone if you need to move from your table. • Be punctual to the session. • Use kind language and do not use curse words. • Put your phones away for the session. • Do not run around unless instructed to. • Do not take any photos without permission. • It is your choice to participate in any of the activities. • If you are not participating please be respectful to those who are. • Help one another throughout the session. • Enjoy!

Keep things simple

Sometimes when we embark on something new we find ourselves with a wealth of creative ideas, which can quickly become overwhelming. Keep your activities simple so that everybody can participate and be flexible in your approach. An activity that you think may take 20 minutes could end up taking double this as people interact, so build an adaptable approach into your work and be less focussed on getting through a list of requirements. The older people are likely to be in attendance as they see a social value to attending the session and children will see this as a treat that takes them away from their usual classroom experience. If you are incorporating craft activities, keep these simple with only a few steps to follow to make the different products. This helps those with limited mobility, and those more able can spend additional time colouring in and designing their crafts further.

In 2021, the grocery chain Sainsbury's undertook a survey of 2,000 participants and found that only 28 per cent of UK families ate a family meal together in the evenings. In research commissioned by "The Big Lunch Campaign" (Eden Project Communities, 2017) it was found that one in four people over the age of 55 are most likely to regularly eat alone. The research, undertaken by the University of Oxford, also found that the more often people eat together, the more likely they are to feel satisfied and happy with their lives. Eating with others promotes togetherness and is a social action that many will miss in later life. Including a snack time in your session, where tea, juice and biscuits can be shared, turns spaces into informal gatherings where people feel able to converse and get to know one another better, so factor this into your plans and budget.

Example planning sheet

Table 10.4 Example planning sheet

Area to consider:	Plan:	Actions:
Name of project:		
Purpose of project:		
How will the project bring mutual benefit?		
Learning objectives:		
Who will be participating and what ages will they be?		
How will you recruit participants and how many people do you require?		
What space will you use for your project?		
What do you see as the main barriers to the project?		
How long will your project run for (both sessions and length of full project)?		
What accessibility considerations do you need to plan for?		
What is the budget for your project and how will this be spent?		
How will you evaluate your project?		
In what ways will you celebrate and publicise the project?		

Identify roles

Intergenerational sessions are easy when everyone understands their roles and responsibilities. Being clear from the outset of the expectations helps to make sure that everything is covered that needs to be and that all health and safety requirements are maintained. This may include areas such as setting up the space, sending out information, planning the activities but also needs to include explaining to pupils and staff their role throughout the session. Be clear to explain the purpose of the session and their role in listening and interacting with others. Older people will not return if they are ignored or there is not a mutual learning exchange so ensure to explain to pupils the instructions for the activities and the importance of them sharing their knowledge and ideas with others. Remember to have people's contact details to hand on the day so you can ensure you have the correct means to get in touch with people if there are any changes to the schedule.

All of us within education can appreciate that there are always lots of hidden jobs that can be forgotten as we progress through activities. If the same people are always left to tidy up or set up the session they will soon become irritated with the project and lose interest. Consider how you will introduce a rota system to not only make it fair to all but also so that everyone can experience the sessions with a fresh perspective. This will help to generate new ideas and allow students to understand the different processes that are needed to incorporate intergenerational experiences into settings.

Planning checklist example

This template will support you on the day to reflect on who has to complete what during the session.

Table 10.5 Example of planning checklist

Action/activity:	Who is responsible:	Complete:

Prepare in advance

Throughout my career, I have observed many students in their Early Years practice and feel incredibly satisfied when I have seen resources prepared in advance that allow for children not to be distracted in their task and the educator able to focus on their learning, rather than where a resource might be. From snacks to worksheets, ensure to include time in your schedule the week before the session to go over final checks and incorporate into the diary time just before people arrive to prepare the environment, to make sure it is set up properly for a warm welcome. As we have considered throughout this book, communication is key to a successful project and you do not want to be off searching for a glue stick when there are important learning opportunities to be a part of!

Adopting a flexible approach

Although planning in advance is very important to provide a structure to your intergenerational project, you will need to be responsive to the cues that you observe and adapt plans according to the response of individuals. Flexibility promotes a sense of calmness within the session and gives you the opportunity to learn from the conversations that take place. Have a bank of resources: if activities are completed quicker than you expected this will help you to hold people's attention and extend learning in different ways. A good way to hold focus is to collect photos from your local area throughout the decades with open questions left on the table as conversation starters. You may also want to include resources relevant to the topic theme you are covering within the project in a similar format, in order to prompt discussions and take this as your lead in how you will progress the programme.

Evaluate your project

We will cover in detail how to evaluate your project within Chapter 12 but remember this is a crucial element for ensuring your project becomes a sustainable part of your educational environment. Use the evaluations to inform your future sessions and gather evidence of what has gone well and what you need to develop further. Templates are included within Chapter 12, so use these to help you gather feedback. Remember to include everyone's voice and to be progressive in your practice to make it work well for all of the participants.

Share your news!

When we have good news we should not keep it to ourselves! As we have learnt throughout this book there are a variety of benefits to intergenerational practice and I would encourage anyone involved in it to be an advocate for it being an essential approach for communities and education. By sharing with others, you are also able to show others best practice and support them in developing their own intergenerational learning spaces. Use your school websites and professional social media pages (with prior consent) to showcase the joy that has come from the time together and also promote the approach you have adopted to help others to understand the professionalism and dedication of the Education Team.

Photo and video example permission form

Table 10.6 Photo and video example permission form

_____ are currently running an intergenerational project (Name) that we are looking forward to welcoming *you/*your child to. Throughout the session we will be taking some photographs and videos for promotional projects and to share with other educators. These images will not be shared with any third parties. We would please ask you to review the below return slip with your details to inform us on how your image can be shared. Many thanks, *Name of group.
<ul><li>I do/not give permission for my photograph/video to be shared for promotional purposes.</li><li>I do/not give permission for my photograph/video to be shared within the school.</li><li>I do/not give permission for my photograph/video to be shared by the teachers during external presentations in relation to the project.</li></ul> Signed: _____ Name print: _____ Date: _____

11 Intergenerational practice in action

Within this chapter we will explore three settings in more detail in order to understand the way in which educators have planned for intergenerational learning according to the needs and requirements of the children and curriculums they follow. You will see that the educators have considered their community and what will work for all parties in attendance within their programmes. All of the projects reported that intergenerational experiences brought great benefit not just to the pupils with whom they worked but also to themselves as professionals, in order to deepen their own experiences and learn new approaches to teaching and developing services.

Throughout our work on intergenerational projects we have been able to connect with those working within Health and Social Care. From this, we have increased our knowledge of how to plan learning opportunities for older people and gained a greater appreciation of how their work has enhanced our local area. Whilst reviewing the case studies I hope that this will bring inspiration as to how intergenerational learning may look within your own educational setting.

Intergenerational projects in preschool playgroups

Peatlands Playgroup is a preschool setting that works with three- to five-year-old children in County Armagh, Northern Ireland. They are based on the outskirts of a semi-rural village, alongside the "Cosy Club"; a day centre for local senior people to visit for social activities and friendship. The playgroup is long established and has enjoyed time with the older people who attend the Cosy Club, through activities such as singing Christmas carols, making gifts for the attendees and supporting the club through fundraising activities. The leader of the setting, Estelle Brownlee, wanted to extend the connections between the two groups and developed a programme that saw the children visit the senior people once a month, where both parties could participate in crafts, snacks and friendship.

The team worked collaboratively with the leaders from the Cosy Club to develop a programme that worked for both parties and shared their resources to keep the financial costs down. It was very important to the team that

DOI: 10.4324/9781003262688-12

the visits would enhance the preschool curriculum that they deliver, and they reviewed their long-term plans to understand how they could plan play opportunities that were relevant to the children's learning which also met with the needs of the Cosy Club attendees. One of the reasons for the success of the programme was that both settings kept the structure very simple. Children would arrive and there was time for the children and older people to introduce themselves, and conversation would take place around a snack time. Activities were kept as table-top play with the resources ready in advance and both the preschool and Cosy Club staff would sit alongside the attendees and participate in the different elements of the session. The leader, Estelle, told me that the hardest part was ensuring that all of the settings policies and procedures for off-site visits were maintained, and it was important to work with the inspecting authorities in advance to plan for this accordingly. Thorough risk assessments and appropriate supervision were maintained throughout on both sides of the collaboration and the playgroup team worked very closely with their parents and carers to ensure they were fully aware of the different events and what the children were participating in. Parents' feedback was very positive. There was not just excitement from the children in the morning when they knew they were going to the Cosy Club, but the parents also took part in this with delight, sharing stories with the team on the conversations at home on the children's time visiting their friends across the road. Estelle found the project a great asset to the children's learning not just because it was a way to extend the children's learning around their curriculum, but also because it extended their learning around the community in which they live and brought new connections with people that they probably would not meet in usual circumstances. It was a great way to connect two groups that had been physically very close together but who had had very little interaction prior to this point.

I got the opportunity to visit the setting on one of their event days and there was a wealth of excitement from children as they bundled up into their coats and boots to head across the road to see their friends. The older residents had already arrived at the Club and children sat between them at the table where the team had previously set up the activities for the day. On this occasion, the craft was making Christmas pictures and this followed the topic that the children had been working on over the last couple of weeks. It felt very different to the usual carol singalong that tends to take place when children visit senior spaces at Christmas and I could observe the relationships that had already formed from prior visits together.

There was a lot of anticipation about the biscuits on offer at the Cosy Club and they may have contained a little more sugar than the usual healthy snack that was had at the playgroup, but this was definitely very exciting for the children and triggered my own memories of the treats my grandmothers used to give me when my parents were out of the way! The older and younger attendees engaged in expansive conversations. Some of the adults participated in the craft, some helped the children and others chose to observe and enjoy their tea as the children played, but all showed happiness at the children's presence and it was lovely to be able to observe what this brought to everyone in attendance.

As we progressed through the morning, there was a moment that will stay with me forever: one of the gentlemen got up and sat down at a keyboard that I had not noticed on my arrival. I later learnt that he used to be in a band and travelled between dance halls entertaining many people each week. When he took to the keyboard, the atmosphere was truly beautiful. We all sang Christmas songs, heard old-time classics and the children were in awe of the music and interactions from the older people. Music makes us all feel young, it takes us back to moments that brought us happiness and the singing felt good for the soul. Up until that moment the gentleman had been very quiet, but the music changed everything. I left the setting that day feeling so content, and I hope that those same feelings were felt by the children and senior people that were present.

Leader Estelle Brownlee told me that recently one of the children who was part of the first year of this programme had come with her mother to collect his younger sibling and pointed out to his mum the Cosy Club on the other side of the car park. He got incredibly excited and told her that was where he used to go for biscuits and spoke about some of the people who he had become friends with. It had been three years since he had been at the playgroup and it felt very significant to Estelle that it was that part of his time with them that he had highlighted to his mother. For a child, the link to the best biscuits is very often a fond memory to reflect on but what it also meant to Estelle was that his time linking with older residents from the community had given him a significant marker in his time within his Early Years setting and a moment that would stay with him for a long time. As Early Years Educators we often accept that children's time with us is forgotten as they progress up into primary school, so it was significant for the child to recall this memory on that day. We do not know where this may lead in the future but it was a connection that the group of children before him would have missed out on and the building would not have attracted any attention. They had changed the building across the road into one that symbolised connection, friendship and learning.

Intergenerational programmes in nursery schools

Windmill Nursery sits on the outskirts of a small town in Northern Ireland. Overlooking a lough, the natural elements of the environment complement the outdoor learning approach that teacher Kierna Corr practices within her provision. For many of their families, the most accessible way to travel to the nursery is by car and it is quite a considerable walk to the nearest shops and amenities. Further along the road is a care home and Kierna and her team initially started their intergenerational journey by visiting this home with the children to share songs and performances with the residents. The care home manager asked if they could develop this into a sustainable project and they began monthly play visits to enable the children and older people to develop relationships and enjoy time together.

Kierna explains that there was a lot of excitement within both groups when the monthly trip was imminent. In order to maintain appropriate supervision levels, parents were rotated to attend the visit with the children and walk them to the home; a beneficial way to include parents and carers into nursery life and get to know families further. Kierna tells me that she has been asked recently by a previous parent if the sessions are able to start again soon post-Covid-19 restrictions, as she hoped to join again as she had gained so much from her participation. It shows the strength of involving families from the outset and opening up opportunities for them to gain an insight into their children's learning experiences.

The learning started from the outset of the session and the walk to the care home allowed for children to explore their local community. Kierna and I discussed how important it is for people to be visible for relationships to develop. Both settings sit behind fences, the roads make it difficult for the young or old to walk a considerable distance, and we reflected on how so very often the youth and senior members of our society become invisible to wider society. Becoming more connected encourages communities to care and love one another and begins to break down some of the prejudices that others may have regarding certain sections of society. Alongside that, the fresh air and contentment of seeing the beautiful lough across from the nursery brings a lot to the children and they take great pleasure from their walk to the care home.

When they arrive at the care home for their sessions, the children are welcomed into the residents' room and play activities are placed out by the activity coordinators who work there. The session is not forced and it is up to both children and older people to participate as they please. Kierna explains that some of the children were quite shy at first as they were not used to the environment or being in the presence of older people, but after a few sessions this shyness dissolved as they got used to their surroundings and developed relationships with others. There are some experiences that stand out in Kierna's mind from previous sessions and she recalls one resident who they'd been told rarely moved from their chair, only to then participate in physical games of "catch" with the children. One of the residents was living with depression and the monthly visit saw a huge change in their mental health both during the session and in the run-up to it. They asked when the children were visiting and found happiness from their interactions with the children. It brought mutual benefit and Kierna tells me about a child who would visit an elderly neighbour with their parents and was very nervous about interacting with them. Following two sessions within the care home, the mother shared with Kierna that their child was responding differently and now went into the neighbour's house with confidence and had begun initiating conversations and building a relationship with them. In a short timescale, both parties had gained learning and social and emotional benefit from their time participating in the intergenerational exchange.

The gratitude from the care home has been humbling for Kierna. They have named a room after the school and it is filled with framed drawings from the children. Having the care home in such close proximity has made the sessions run smoothly and Kierna is very grateful for the strong relationships with parents who are able to support the project. The cost of running the programme has been limited as there has been no extra expense for the nursery, and Kierna explains that there would be some cost to the care home for providing snacks and activities for the children and older people to enjoy. The care home manager has valued this connection greatly and did not see this small cost as a barrier, instead focussing on the benefits of young and old spending time together.

Kierna has gained a wealth of experience internationally in her educational professional development and discusses the sadness of seeing groups segregated from one another. She recalls some time spent in Sweden, where she observed how apartments were designed so that older people live on the ground floor, families on the first floor and those more physically able to manage the stairs on higher floors. We agreed that in Northern Ireland we tend to segregate age groups and this leads to higher levels of prejudice and an "out of sight, out of mind" mentality. Over the Covid-19 lockdown restrictions, Kierna talks about the positives of having had these sessions previously as it reminded families to stay in touch with the care homes through letters and cards. Kierna and the team are committed to getting the sessions back up and running as soon as it is safe to do so, as she feels it is not just the children and seniors who gained from this experience, but also the staff, and it became a real highlight of their monthly calendar.

The experience opened up the opportunity for children to see different emotions, to begin to develop empathy with others and also to understand that we do not all look and behave the same. It also encouraged children to understand that even with differences, there are a variety of attributes and experiences that connect us. From this young age, children were able to develop empathy and care for others through the project.

Intergenerational projects in schools

Set up in Holy Cross Catholic Church parish hall in Catford, London, the "Diamond Club" began its journey over 20 years ago as a community space for older people, and from their early stages links were made with Holy Cross Primary School. In close proximity to both the church and the school, generations came together within the three spaces and the initial connection came from attendees of the Diamond Club being invited to shows and performances put on by the school and the church. With over 60 attendees in the senior group, there are a number of activities to bring people together and enjoy social experiences. Lesley Allen, who has been working with the Diamond Club since it was established, tells me that the performances brought a lot of happiness to people who were maybe unable to see their own grandchildren or simply wanted to enjoy the celebrations that came from the events. The primary school children also engaged well, eager to meet new friends with whom they could share their performances.

From this, greater engagement came from the generations when out within the community, and children and adults would stop for chats with one another. It was felt by those that worked in the Diamond Club and the Holy Cross Primary School teachers that it would be a natural process to formalise the links further and explore setting up intergenerational sessions between the two settings. Lesley would meet with the head teacher on a termly basis to plan out sessions that brought mutual benefit. From her meetings with the head teacher, Lesley and the teachers set up sessions at both the school and the Diamond Club building.

Lesley tells me about a show that was put on by both groups whereby songs were exchanged. Children performed songs such as "The White Cliffs of Dover" whilst senior attendees performed pop songs by singers such as Jesse James which they had been taught during the intergenerational programme. I am able to see the happiness from Lesley that comes from sharing this experience and the treat that came for the ticketed audience. The show challenged perceptions, with the two age groups singing songs from the other generation's era and Lesley reflects on how much delight it brought everyone. Reminiscence sessions and sharing skills such as knitting brought deeper connection and a mutual space for young and old to learn together, learning skills that might be lost if not learnt from our older generations.

A highlight of the year for both parties was the annual tea parties for children that were leaving the primary school that year. This provided an opportunity for questions to be posed about moving on and gratitude for what had been. Senior attendees' experiences of transitions provided children with reassurance as they prepared to move onto somewhere new. Lesley reflects on the excitement from the children of a "formal" event to mark the occasion and the discussions over the formalities of things such as pouring from a teapot, something some of the children had not tried before. It is evident to see the connections between children's curriculum and experiences within the activities and how this type of curriculum enhances it further, whilst building on children's confidence and emotional development.

The project extended when curriculums were encouraged to recognise the value of play for children's development. A link with the nursery school was developed and eight senior members would go to play with the children's resources alongside them. Lesley explains that for this aspect of their practice they decided an emphasis on flow was needed and nothing was forced. Activities such as sand, water and sensory play were set up and participants played alongside each other, engaging in conversation. The "messy" play was something that the senior residents really enjoyed as it was not something in which they would usually participate and Lesley recalls the smiles that came from the older people on their return from the sessions. Due to the Covid-19 lockdown periods of 2020 and 2021, this activity unfortunately had to be put on hold, but the connections between the two establishments were maintained through pre-recorded video exchanges and letters between the participants.

The proximity of the sites brought the great benefit of being able to run a vast number of sessions, along with the positive relationship of staff between the Diamond Club at Holy Cross Church and Holy Cross Primary School. Lesley explains there are a diverse mix of attendees within the club and some attendees have dementia and other needs that need to be considered. Lesley talks about the importance of schools being aware that sometimes conversations may not always follow the patterns that we expect. Communicating and building strong relationships with parents and carers have provided time to explain this and gain an understanding that their children may be exposed to some language and discussion that would not normally take place within an educational setting. Through this transparency and the professionalism of the teachers and Diamond Club staff, this has been fully understood with an appreciation from families of the activities they are planning.

From the Diamond Club, Lesley has set up another club to bring communities together including the "Bring me Sunshine Club" which organises 12 performance events throughout the year. A local dance academy approached the club to ask if they could do a show together and from this a performance called "Down Memory Lane" was created. The show saw an 86-year-old take to the stage and it is wonderful to hear Lesley share both the joy this brought to the individual as well as their disbelief that they had been able to sing in front of a crowd of 180 people. Intergenerational events can help to develop people's confidence to share their talents and boost their self-confidence. The intergenerational approach encouraged people who would not normally perform to be on centre stage, and the outcome was clearly magnificent.

In order to return to face-to-face activities following the Covid-19 pandemic, Lesley and the school are now developing a new idea. It is a reminder of the need to be responsive and adaptive within our plans in order to suit the needs of individuals and organisational procedures. Lesley tells me that the Diamond Club holds a weekly Zumba exercise for the seniors in the morning and it was thought this would be a useful time for those who did not want to participate to gain some time with the children from the school. They are now introducing playground walks where seniors and primary children can walk together within the playground and enjoy company, alongside connecting with the natural world. This is a great way to encourage conversations and sharing of knowledge, whilst meeting the requirements of restricted indoor activities and improving the emotional health of individuals through the time spent outdoors.

This is not the only activity under development and Lesley shares how the group connected with their local sixth form college during the lockdown period, with Christmas goody bags being put together by students for the attendees of the Diamond Club. This relationship is one that the club would like to develop further in the future and they have visitors come in to spend time with them through the Duke of Edinburgh Award Scheme and they also have a young writer who supports their newsletter, submitting a "words of positivity" article each month. This not only connects them through the regular feature, but also gives the young author the opportunity to strengthen her curriculum vitae and showcase her work when applying for jobs. This openness and determination to build on their local community evidences how all areas of education can engage with intergenerational practice and how activities can be implemented to suit the individual needs of the attendees. Teenagers have taught the Diamond Club attendees how to use technology and new equipment, in exchange for knowledge on a variety of different areas. That mutual benefit is what has helped to make this project a success.

Returning to our conversation about the school links, the widespread activities that have been completed over the years shows how both parties organising the programme reflect on the needs of both generations, in order to create mutual benefit and meet with the expectations of the school and club. There have been history projects put in place to link the Year 4 pupils with the club to support the children's curriculum and in turn brought older generations the time to share their experiences and pass this on to the next generation to bring forward their stories and bring the curriculum to life.

Lesley sees many benefits from the work that they have completed together with the schools and puts great emphasis on how this has always been mutual across the generations. Older attendees have expressed feeling more positive towards young children and recognise that young people are happy individuals that have good things to share, breaking down the negative perceptions that they previously had of that generation. The sharing of technology skills offered an opportunity to connect, which was uplifting and became a fun activity to do together, reducing the anxiety of trying something new. Lesley notes that having a good time is an essential part of the programme and that the sessions bring a bit of joy to people's lives, something many who are feeling isolated or lonely have been lacking within their lives. Located within the Borough of Lewisham, Lesley has seen how the local mayor has advocated the work that they do and promotes intergenerational practice in order to make the borough a more age-friendly society. Practically, the links between community organisations have opened up opportunities for new funding avenues, supporting the club in its sustainability.

Intergenerational projects in colleges

Shirley-Anne McAdam works as a Lecturer in Further and Higher education in County Tyrone, Northern Ireland. She has been involved in intergenerational learning for the past five years and used her practice as the basis of her research for her degree in Early Childhood Studies. She now supports others completing their own research in this area and has found the opportunity to be involved in intergenerational programmes a rewarding and beneficial process, both as an academic and also for the happiness that it has brought to her work. Initially the intergenerational sessions were an add-on to students' curriculum and she supported Level Three, post-16 students in running monthly events that brought young and older attendees together. Through her research she observed how the project was not only supporting the literacy, social and emotional development of the primary school children who attended, but also saw how it was enhancing the Further Education students' work and emotional wellbeing. Shirley-Anne McAdam saw the transition to embed intergenerational practice into this programme becoming tailored and that it is now a key part of students' portfolio of evidence towards their qualification. She tells me how it not only boosted the students' confidence but was also an important piece of work that students could include on their university applications, due to the social action focus and doing something different to others who may be applying to similar courses.

Now that intergenerational practice has become a core project for students, Shirley-Anne discusses how much easier it is to run the programmes and give them the time for development that is essential for making the activities sustainable throughout the year.

Students begin the project each year by linking with local care homes through a letter writing exchange. Whilst students prepare these letters, their portfolio of evidence includes their research on the importance of inter-agency and multidisciplinary working for children's development. Although the letter exchanges are a lot of fun, the activity also gives students the opportunity to see the connections to the units they are studying and the importance of collaborative services through their research. Once the students have built up the relationships, people from both primary schools and the care homes are then invited into the college and engage with stimulating activities that are designed by the Early Years students. To link with the curriculum that is being followed, this is backed up by evidence-based practice where students identify how these activities support children's development and how it enhances community and fosters positive experiences and outcomes for children.

Throughout the programme, reflective sessions are run to teach students how to engage in reflective practice appropriately and give them the skills needed to move into their vocational areas. Students are taught a variety of theories of reflection and can then understand how this links to their practice and the most beneficial one to use in relation to the task they are undertaking. Shirley-Anne has seen a number of subject areas engage in the programme and some do this as a one-off session and others for more. The ability to adapt to suit certain subjects is of great benefit, as it allows for the development and utilising of skills and knowledge to be shared.

Within this project, the college had an active Science, Technology, Engineering and Mathematics (STEM) centre that supported children and young people in all aspects of education within this field and provided outreach learning programmes. Shirley-Anne highlights the benefits of being able to collaborate with a different team within the college, who could offer a contrasting and fresh perspective to activities, whilst also enriching the learning that took place across the age groups. Early Years Lecturers shared teaching with those who specialised within the centre and this increased the knowledge of students on how they could extend planning within the Early Years environment, whilst also introducing the primary school children to new areas of curriculum that were not solely focussed on within their own school curriculum. The lecturers found that this collaboration also released some of the burden of lesson planning and were introduced as teaching strategies that they could use within their own practice outside of the project.

One of Shirley-Anne's favourite moments from the project was having her own mother-in-law join in with the sessions alongside students' own families and those of the team she worked with. She feels it brought a greater appreciation of one another and the informal atmosphere allowed for everyone to relax and get to know each other better. Students' minor concerns were shared, which otherwise may not have come up in normal classroom conversations, and Shirley-Anne gained a greater understanding of what students' lives looked like outside of the setting.

12 Evaluating intergenerational projects

Throughout this book, you will have gained the understanding of the purpose of intergenerational practice. Its value and worth are important in order to evaluate how to strengthen provision and understand the benefits it has brought to children and the older generations. A collaborative approach to evaluation should be incorporated into the design of your evaluations; a process that should take place throughout the programme. By evaluating our projects we are able to share our practice and analyse both the successes and the barriers we have faced by recording our findings. By sharing our learning, our projects are able to ripple out to the wider community and support us in raising the profile of the need for intergenerational learning.

There is not a "one size fits all" design to intergenerational programmes. What works for us one year may not work with a different group of people. It is important for us to be reflective and to consider the needs of all those who participate. Evaluating your project will allow you to build on the work that has been done and continue to improve, ensuring that the project brings mutual benefit to the attendees. The evaluation should ensure that everyone's voice shines through in its review; this should not be an activity purely conducted by the facilitators of the project and there are a variety of ways to gain this input.

During our own projects we used both evaluations and research to focus on particular areas of intergenerational practice. You may be working with stakeholders who want to conduct formal or action research that is separate to the main evaluation, and this will be beneficial for further insight for your evaluation. Throughout our project we had research taking place, I myself completed my Master's dissertation focussing on how the project supported children's linguistic development. A colleague completing her BA (Hons) in Childhood and Youth Studies used the space to analyse how the connections impacted on children's social and emotional development and then we had external researchers, both locally and internationally, reviewing the use of intergenerational projects in schools and colleges. Throughout our planning we wanted to ensure that we had open doors to researchers so that we could gain the most from our experience and also have the opportunity to showcase the benefits of intergenerational practice to others. Shirley-Anne McAdam discusses her experience of researching the project for her BA with me and the value it

DOI: 10.4324/9781003262688-13

brought to her own learning and also to those to whom she disseminated her findings and found that it enhanced the student experience as they were able to relate how they could lead particular aspects of the session to support specific areas of children's development, whilst improving links with partner schools.

There can be a number of ways that you can evaluate your project and in order for it to be a beneficial process it is important to clarify from the outset the purpose of your evaluation and to reflect on what you hope to gain from this process. Reflecting both during your sessions and at set times (for example at the end of your programme calendar) allows for discussions to take place to analyse whether the objectives you set were relevant and have been met. It also allows time for review of the practicalities of the activities and to investigate any barriers in order to make your projects sustainable for the future.

This process should not be judgemental and should aim to evidence the strengths of the programme and the individuals involved, alongside reviewing supportive ways to develop further. If your project has been funded, it may be that the evaluation process is a required function to meet with the requirements of the funding, and if this is the case it is important to review their expectations and understand from the outset how you will gather the required evidence. Clear objectives from the beginning of your programme will help you to have clarity on what you hope to achieve and understand how to plan accordingly for this (particularly important when funders are involved in the process).

When undertaking evaluations we should not see these as a report that we complete and file away but one from which we can learn and share accordingly. An ongoing evaluation will support you to gain fresh ideas from those involved and to see things from a different perspective. There may be areas which you thought had gone well but, from reflecting on the evaluation, you realise did not actually suit the needs of the individuals. This is an important area for us to review and allows us to consider how we co-plan with the groups and ensure their voice is embedded into the programmes we facilitate. When the team with whom I worked completed our own evaluations, we saw the value it brought to presenting our work professionally and it gave us clear evidence that could be used by others. We want others to appreciate what we do and it also helps us to build on the need of intergenerational practice as relevant and needed within educational systems.

Throughout all of the time involved in intergenerational practice we must ensure that it is conducted ethically and from a values-based approach, and this includes our evaluation processes. Prior to starting your evaluation, build on the relationships you have within the team and review any pre-conceived ideas that individuals may have. Creating open and honest spaces for discussion allows us to understand the purpose of our evaluation and remove bias within our approach. We will all have our own priorities within the programme and we need to understand how our practice may be influenced by the agenda we bring to the group. Consider these together and how they complement, rather than conflict with, each other. Recording your journey will bring a wealth of mutual understanding to each element of the programme and also provide you with literature to return to in order to consider how you move forward in your development.

Be aware that when evaluating your project, all those involved must be informed of your intentions and what you are doing in advance. When working across age groups, you will gain a great insight into other people's lives and hear a great deal of personal stories. Individuals may feel confident sharing this with you but might not want this shared further so consider this when recording your evaluations. When working with children, it is important that they have also given informed consent to the process, alongside gaining appropriate parent/carer consent. For us, we had our main evaluations to do, alongside the research projects conducted by individuals. This required new consent procedures to be undertaken, and we need to remember that one permission does not guarantee the other.

Our senior participants on the programme were intrigued from the outset by the purpose of our activities. For them to commit to what we were doing it was important for us to be clear of the intentions of the programme and ensure that they were involved in each stage of the process. For them, participating had to bring value and satisfaction to their daily routines and they wanted (quite rightly) to ensure there was no hidden agenda in the work that we were undertaking. Embedding their feedback and voice into our work helped us to develop a programme that worked for them, whilst meeting our own objectives. It also allowed them to see how their involvement would benefit the students' learning and this was something that many were pleased to be involved with, as they saw that their experiences and knowledge could benefit others.

Systems for evaluation

Interviews

It is important for us to remember that the systems that we use within our teams may not suit the participants of the programme. Handing out written evaluation forms can be embarrassing for those who, for example, are unable to use their hands to record their experience, so interviews where you record information can be much more useful throughout the process. It also prevents time being taken away from the session or giving others work to do away from the space. Interviews can also be of great use in order to gain more insight from the children, and questions can be designed to suit the varying ages of participants. Make your intentions clear; if you are asking a question for your evaluation ensure that participants are aware of this so that they understand that their voice will be represented accurately and appropriately. Have your questions agreed in advance, and you may wish to show the questions to participants prior to the interview so that they have more time to reflect on their answers.

Questionnaires

Questionnaires can be a useful tool for gaining insight into people's experiences and can be more useful for the professionals with whom you are working, rather than the participants. Using online questionnaires, with short questions to save on time for those with busy workloads, can be a beneficial way of gaining feedback quickly and allows individuals to complete them at their own convenience. There are also many free tools you can design online for this. I would recommend not waiting until the end of a programme to ask for feedback in this way, but instead ask a couple of questions throughout the project to gather insight as you progress. Always check the accessibility of your evidence-gathering tool to ensure everyone has access, and reflect on how much it is asking of the individual. A short, considered answer is better than no response at all.

Templates for questionnaires

You may wish to use these templates for your projects or use them to give you an idea of how your evaluation questionnaires may look. These have been adapted to suit both children and older participants.

Primary-aged pupils

Table 12.1 Sample questionnaire for primary-aged pupils

We are delighted that you have participated in our intergenerational project with us! So that we can learn more about how to make this programme even better for the future we would like you to complete this form. If you are unsure of how to complete it please ask and be honest in your responses. Thank you!	
Age and class:	
Gender	Boy/Girl
Is this the first intergenerational project you have participated in?	Yes/No
Did you like taking part in the project?	Yes/No
What was the highlight of the project?	
Is there anything you would change about the sessions?	

(continued)

108 *Evaluating intergenerational projects*

Table 12.2 Cont.

Read the following statements and circle your answer:		
Statement:	Yes:	No:
I enjoyed all of the sessions	☺	☹
I found it easy to make friends with the group of adults	☺	☹
I have learnt new things from attending	☺	☹
I feel more confident from participating in the project	☺	☹
I know more about my community now	☺	☹
I would like to do more projects with older people	☺	☹

Post-primary pupils

Table 12.2 Sample questionnaire for post-primary pupils

We are delighted that you have participated in our intergenerational project with us! So that we can learn more about how to make this programme even better for the future we would like you to complete this form. If you are unsure of how to complete it please ask and be honest in your responses, we would appreciate your feedback so consider how we can improve the projects further and what you gained from participating. Thank you!	
Age and class:	
Gender:	
Is this the first intergenerational project you have participated in?	Yes/No
Did you like taking part in the project?	Yes/No

Table 12.2 Cont.

Read the following questions and include your answers alongside these:			
Statement:	Yes:	No:	Comment:
I understood what the project was before participating:	☺	☹	
I enjoyed meeting people a different age to me:	☺	☹	
I think differently about older people now:	☺	☹	
I know more about my community now:	☺	☹	
I enjoyed the different activities:	☺	☹	
I found the environment comfortable to be in:	☺	☹	
I found out new things about different age groups:	☺	☹	
I felt welcomed at every session:	☺	☹	
I thought my voice was listened to at every session:	☺	☹	
I like learning in an intergenerational space:	☺	☹	
I feel I taught the older people new things:	☺	☹	
There are things I would change if doing it again:	☺	☹	

Participants post-school age

Table 12.3 Sample questionnaire for post school-aged participants

We appreciate you participating in our intergenerational project and hope that it brought you as much as it did us. We would really appreciate your feedback to support us in building on our intergenerational work and design our programmes to suit all those who attend. Please be honest in your feedback as it will support us in our improvements moving forward. Thank you for your time!	
Age bracket (please circle):	18–25 | 25–44 | 45–64 | 65–79 | 80–90 | 90+
Please share with us your current housing accommodation (please circle):	Living independently | Living with spouse | Living with my extended family | Supported living housing | Residential care

Please read the following questions and add your responses:

Statement:	Yes (Please tick):	No (Please tick):	Comment:
I have participated in intergenerational programmes before:			
I understood the purpose of the project before attending:			
I attended for the social side of the project:			
I attended as I wanted to learn something new from younger people:			
I enjoyed spending time with different age groups:			
I felt I had something to offer to the younger participants:			

Table 12.3 Cont.

The environment was welcoming and met with my needs:			
I now feel differently about younger people:			
My voice was heard during the sessions:			
I was able to participate in the different activities:			
The timings of the programme suited my routine:			
I learnt new things from participating in the programme:			
I feel less isolated from participating the project:			
I believe this is something our community benefits from:			
I would participate in future intergenerational projects:			

Drawings

Younger children may find it difficult to understand questionnaires but gathering their feedback using creative avenues can be very beneficial for gaining their perspectives. You may wish to incorporate a drawing session towards the end of your project and sit alongside the children, gathering their anecdotal conversations as they progress through designing their artwork. Consider what you hope to achieve from this activity. You may want to use questions as prompts, such as:

- *What was your favourite part of our programme?*
- *Can you draw a picture of you with the friends you made during our project?*
- *Why has the project been different to what you normally do at nursery?*
- *Will you draw a picture of your favourite part of being together during our sessions?*

Thinking rounds

Nancy Kline (2009) discusses how her thinking-round techniques can be used to empower individuals to think *well* and encourages us to consider how the quality of everything we do depends on the quality of what we do first. Thinking rounds require us to leave our ego behind and not interrupt others' thinking, taking it in turns to discuss openly what our freshest thinking is in relation to a subject area. This was an evaluative technique that we used throughout our programmes with students, so we could generate new ideas and hear their freshest thinking on what we should change, or adapt, in order to enhance the programme. It also generated discussion on how it related to their course learning outcomes, inspiring them to take the lead on designs of their portfolios of evidence and college experiences.

Within thinking rounds, time is set aside where there will be no interruptions and everyone has the opportunity to speak. As you move from one person to the next it is vitally important that people do not jump in whilst someone else is sharing their freshest thinking on the area of focus, but wait for the individual to pass onto the next person in the group. It is important to wait your turn and to take a pause to collect your thoughts as you listen to others speaking. Individuals' feelings are important to acknowledge and it is important to stress beforehand that this is a safe space in which they can be honest. This will support the evaluative process as you will be able to gain a true perspective of the experiences of others. This strategy can also be used in pairs and can be a valuable method of thinking through the different areas of the programme so that pairs can give feedback to the main group.

What happens if something has not worked?

Not all of the projects that are planned will run smoothly and there may be a range of barriers that lead to programmes not working as effectively as you had hoped. In my own experience, there was times when care home staff were off sick and this impacted on travel arrangements for senior members travelling to us, and when the Covid-19 pandemic hit the feeling of loss when forced to cancel our monthly sessions was devastating. All of us gained so much from the time together and we knew how valuable it was to connect with one another. If you find that a programme has not run as smoothly as you had hoped, do not be deterred! Your evaluations will allow you to appreciate what you need to do to adapt your plans and ensure that it is then tailored to suit the needs of your attendees and pupils. When the Covid-19 pandemic required us to go into lockdown we looked to new ways to connect as we knew that our existing model would not work for the world we were living in. A completely new approach was adopted where we connected via letter exchanges, videos and video conference mechanisms. It was not something that we wanted to continue on a long-term basis but it gave us the ability to improve our ICT skills together and maintain the links that we had built up over the years. If something is not working for you, or you feel the stress of it falling on an individual's shoulders, it is important to take a step back as a team and evaluate how you can move forward to redesign your programme to ensure that it works for everyone. It is vital to remember that this style of learning relies on people, and we all come with our own perspectives, agendas and expectations. What looks good on paper may not work in reality. Reflecting, and acting, will be a core skill that needs to be developed by those invested in implementing the activities, and open lines of communication will support you in making your project sustainable. Regularly revisiting your intended outcomes will ensure that you are meeting the requirements for your curriculum, whilst developing intergenerational learning exchanges.

13 Social action and shifting perspectives

The fast-paced nature of society often leaves us missing out on the beauty of living in the moment. Older generations have many years on our children and their experiences can bring us the gift of seeing life from a new perspective and appreciating that we do not all have many years ahead of us so need to embrace the moments as they come. Our society is fearful of old age and what comes next; intergenerational time together allows us the time to feel at ease with who we are and appreciate the time ahead of us. Throughout my time on intergenerational projects, the gift of having an older person having the time to connect and appreciate being together has brought a warmth that I have not felt elsewhere in my practice. Both children and young people within our societies are marginalised and often invisible in how we shape our communities; it is now that we need to reflect on how we make education and wider support services more inclusive for all, where we break down assumptions and build environments where we can fully bring ourselves forward.

The world is so much more accessible nowadays. Children and young people have the ability to travel and study abroad, with a vast array of educational and future job prospects available to them. However, we owe it to them to build communities where they see local opportunities and feel themselves valued as an active member of society. When our children look at their local area, do they think, "This is where I want to grow old?", or do they see it as a place they are desperate to flee? Intergenerational learning environments bring us an opportunity to connect our communities and show children and young people that there is a place for them as they grow older. Throughout my life my "family" has been made up of those who have shown me care and love rather than blood relations, and for many of us without family in close proximity we can still gain that thoughtfulness that comes from spending time across the generations and making new friends who will be there for us, listening to what we have to say. Reflecting back on the Blackfoot Community Framework in Chapter 1, we are aware of the need to feel connected in order to thrive.

During one of our intergenerational programmes, children, teenagers and seniors worked together to review their local area and how they used it. It was interesting and intriguing that all age groups discussed similar locations within the town and their inaccessibility and how they wanted these areas to be regenerated. The older attendees told us stories of how areas were used when they were growing up, and we enjoyed hearing how one of the local loughs had been used for ice skating and summer swims. The lough now sits behind fencing and I am sure is a risk none of us would want for our children but as the lady told us about her memories of the space, she told us how important it was for the young people to have accessibility to leisure activities within the area such as the ice skating she remembered so fondly. She was determined this would go into our plan for improving our community even though it was not an activity that she would now use. Within that moment, the younger participants saw that there were others who would push the agenda for them, and it was a significant point in our programme where they got to see that older people wanted a better society for them to enjoy and connect with.

Our plans for the local area tried to be realistic with some *maybe* hopeful ideas for our community. There was consideration given to strategic benches put along roads so that older people could rest and manage longer walks and also have the opportunity to sit beside others for a chat. Participants identified areas where they felt safe and secure and considered how these could be developed further in order to make them mutual spaces for all age groups. Seeing our community through the eyes of a variety of ages gave us a better understanding of one another and what was important to us. We opened the doors of these sessions to our local council and it was great to see their representation. They listened to what everyone had to say and got to see first-hand the drawings, plans and discussions that took place to develop our area. What was most important was they took this back to their council offices and shared it with others, and we engaged with a follow-up evaluation on the improvements that could be made. This went into development plans for the area and we are now seeing changes being implemented. How often do children and senior citizens gain the opportunity to directly impact on decisions made on community planning? Particularly those in social isolation and who are not engaged with community groups.

Where many of us saw the lockdown period as an opportunity for a fresh approach to community building, we found ourselves more divided than ever. Our young people are seeing the destruction of our planet, the harm it is causing for future generations. Sadly, the community spirit embraced at the start of 2020 seems to have waned, and at the time of writing we are seeing those in the most senior positions of power demonstrating destructive and ego-centric behaviours that do not take into account the feelings and needs of others. Our children and young people see this and I know from experience that they want something better. We need to provide them with chances to learn the skills to be innovative, caring leaders who adopt values and person-centred approaches. Intergenerational learning is a way of embedding this into your schools and learning environments. You are able to explore important topics with people who have diverse experiences and knowledge.

A surefire way to get all of the family together is when a new David Attenborough documentary is released. My eldest daughter once shared with me a vast amount of knowledge on climate change and she told me she had watched one of his programmes on her phone, gaining a greater understanding of the love that our planet needs. It made me realise that she sought out those who would provide her with true and accurate information and wanted to know more about making our planet better for others. Ageism comes as we grow older and are influenced by the cultural assumptions around us. The more time we spend learning and listening to those who have lived the research, job roles and life experience, the more able we are to design structures and opportunities that not only put a focus on people but also on our natural environment. As an educator, I do not have all the answers and by expanding the number of mentors and speakers I bring into the learning environment, the more knowledge and expertise I will be able to share with the students. Using an informal setting also supports us in removing the power dynamics between teachers and pupils.

We all have a tendency to look back with nostalgia. Baby-boomers were able to walk into employment straight from school, they had the ability to secure mortgages to buy their own homes and they did not find themselves with the crippling debt of many nowadays. This leaves a bitter taste in the mouths of the next generation at the fact that things have got worse rather than better; a sense that life has been made worse for those starting out in adult life. Our blame culture is at the forefront of our minds: if it wasn't for them, life would be better for us. Without honest and open discussions we are unable to move past the assumption that life was easier for others. The same can be said for the views of older people on the young, and as you progress through intergenerational learning you will observe that these assumptions lessen and people start to see things differently. You have the ability to provide spaces where we can build respect, trust and understanding; important attributes that remove anger and allow us to move forward as a strong community.

Throughout the day we are bombarded with images of how we should look, feel and present ourselves to others. We flick through social media and the images show us unrealistic targets for our different roles and responsibilities. Alongside this, there is the focus on staying youthful. The pressure is seen throughout the day on the magazine counter, the computer pop-up ads and television advertisements. The *anti-ageing* industry has boomed over the last few decades and continues to grow, with forecasters predicting that between 2021 and 2026 there will be an approximate 29.8 per cent increase in an industry that is already worth 43.2 million pounds sterling (Statista, 2022). This is not just for females; the male anti-ageing industry is also on the rise. Alex Moshakis (2019) discussed the need for men to stay young and fit due to age discrimination impacting on career opportunities. Western society's fixation on youthfulness makes it difficult for us to love ourselves for who we are and not embrace the new stages of life as we progress. How many times have you looked into the mirror and studied the frown lines that have etched onto your face over the years? Do we observe the stories that lie behind them or instead look back with a desire to return to our youth? How much better would life be if we saw the stories, remembered the nights of laughter that have brought the indents around the eyes; smile at the years of frowning at our children who were taught principles with a raised brow. Recognise that we are still here living in this moment, despite the nights that have left our eyes weary. It is ingrained in our culture to maintain youth at all costs. Our children see this, and what values does that teach them in relation to older generations? Our fear of looking (and becoming) older comes at a cost as to how we view others and how we view ourselves.

The World Health Organization's report on ageism (2021) identified a need for greater data on ageism and how to reduce it. Through the projects that we run, we are in a key position to gather information and evaluate this, sharing it with the policy makers around us. Action research provides educators with the opportunity to deepen and develop their skills and also brings data and knowledge that can be shared in an accessible and productive manner.

Within any educational project, it works most effectively when led by the individuals engaged in the programme. Sarah McCully Russell from Linking Generations has been involved in the development of intergenerational champions and explains that they really wanted to focus on young people taking on this role rather than the teachers or other adults who had been involved. Intergenerational champions would act as an advocate for explaining the role and value to others of intergenerational learning, promoting its benefits and clearly explaining how they had participated in intergenerational connections within their educational experience. Young people's voices being heard is really important for confidence building and self-esteem. It is incredibly powerful for a student to see that they have influenced change and through these activities they are developing the skills needed for future employment and career progression. They will also carry intergenerational practice with them into the future, recognising the potential and need to bring people together to tackle social isolation and support those in less fortunate positions.

As you progress in your intergenerational programmes I would encourage you to look down at your feet, as well as towards the horizon. Throughout your programmes you will be focussing on the individuals who are participating – appreciate that focus and be in the moment to reflect in action on the benefits that it brings. As you continue with your reflections, consider how you can share, support others and bring change not just within your own organisation, but also in the wider structures. Throughout the intergenerational projects I have been involved in, I saw the way they influenced others and the positive outcomes that came from our openness. Policy makers are starting to recognise the value of intergenerational experiences, and you can be the grassroots initiative that encourages more to become involved. Small ripples make great waves. Be the change and move forward with love and compassion, committing to making our communities and educational settings better for both our children and older people.

Conclusion

My first plans for intergenerational practice were heavily influenced by my own childhood experiences. Growing up in a predominately female family, my two grandmothers played a significant part in shaping my values and outlook for the rest of my life. In our first intergenerational session at a Further Education college, I did not want to take away from the students' lead, but I did want to ensure we offered a warm welcome to the visitors who had come to participate in the day's activities. Thanks to some technological wizards at the college I was able to do my welcome in cartoon format and I recorded "Cartoon Fey's" voiceover, with words that told part of the story of my nana and the important role she had played in my life. It was important for me that all of us recognised that the session was so very much about building relationships.

I was recently struck by the true value of sitting at my nana's feet and listening to her stories as my own eldest daughter moves onto a new stage in life and enters university life. Our daughter is exploring her values in this new chapter, phoning home to chat about the informal moral code which we have taught her and how it fits within the wider world. It is through storytelling that we are able to share with her how that has helped us within our own lives and experiences. Our nana had many stories but there are a few that I asked her to share over and over again when I was a child, listening intently and aware of each stage of the story as the rhythm of words flowed from her. Growing up in the Docklands of London, she was born into a crammed, busy family home. When she was born she was placed in the cot alongside a little baby boy, and his mother turned to her mother and told her, "Your baby will make a fine wife for my baby Robert one day". My great-grandmother predicted it from the start and the two babies grew up to fall head over heels in love. Even in her eighties, when she had lost him over 40 years earlier, following a heart attack on their belated honeymoon, I felt the love she had for him surround and comfort me as I listened to her recall their time together. Nana did not live a sheltered life. She drove lorries across Europe during the Second World War, not only delivering the essential supplies needed for the war effort, but also smuggling stockings, tobacco, lipstick and even diamonds across borders. I would watch my parents cringe as she told the story "There was one time I thought I killed a man" and she would go on to share how a soldier had tried to force her to

DOI: 10.4324/9781003262688-15

become intimate with him and she kicked him so hard he dropped like a rock. She went back to her sergeant who she begged to go back and check on him. He returned with a chuckle. The man was hurt, very hurt, along with his ego, and the sergeant told her that he did not expect the soldier to make the same mistake again. The story may not have been appropriate for a young child but it showed me her strength, and it taught me not to make presumptions about others' power over me.

When I was born, Nana was proactive in leading social action initiatives in her local community. I shared my nana with the majority of Deptford market and I would watch in awe as people from all generations would stop her for a cuddle and a chat. Her work in organising boat trips for children with disabilities through the Deptford carnival fundraisers led to one of her proudest moments of meeting Princess Diana, and the whole family received a copy of the kind letter that the Princess sent following her visit.

But it was only in this last month that I recognise some of the hidden stories that Nana felt unable to share as easily. Nana was an intelligent individual who won a scholarship to a local grammar school. This was a huge deal for someone within the working-class areas of the Docks. Her parents found a grant for the school uniform and she was ready to progress up the class ladder into new opportunities. That was until her parents realised that there was an additional fee of a shilling a week for napery and the family were unable to afford it. Instead of the grammar school education that she had hoped for, Nana quickly moved through school without the same chances that could have been. The

Figure C.1 Nana with her three great-grandchildren and granddaughter Fey a week before she sadly passed away. Photo by author.

deep appreciation I have for how hard she worked to progress her family cannot be described in words. She laid the way for my mother to go on to her grammar school scholarship, for me to gain a Higher Education and for my eldest daughter to now be the first of us to directly follow school with a university place. We will never understand that struggle, we will never hear my great-grandmother's pleas, begging my nana not to be taken to hospital in case she ended up in the workhouse left to rot like so many of her friends and family had in the past. What we do carry forward though are those working-class values that taught us everything we needed to push ourselves, love our neighbours and step up to support one another within our communities. Whenever I was with Nana, nobody was ever excluded.

When my own father died when I was a teenager, my nana was the only one to fully show her understanding of my feelings. This is not to belittle the other support I had around me; her experience of life allowed for the grief that surrounded her to be shared in a more practical way than those feeling the harsh sadness of loss alongside me. As we grow older, we sadly experience more grief as we lose family and friends along the way and her spiritual aura brought me the ability to feel love at a time when I was determined to push it away due to the sadness I was battling. Her experiences allowed her to share a wealth of coping mechanisms. She would bring me slices of white bread slathered in real butter and actively listen, sharing her own emotional responses in a way that taught me real empathy and understanding of others. She never judged my outbursts as I rebelled in my teenage years following the grief, instead giving me a space to explore these new feelings that I could not understand.

The sharing of this story may feel slightly indulgent; it moves away from the practical aspects of intergenerational practice but it is also one of the most important stories I can share. To record our history, we have to write our story. Through your intergenerational projects you have the opportunity to collate and share the greatest gift of storytelling. A gift that allows us to understand our heritage, learn of the heritage of others and gain the wisdom of those that come before us. There are stories that bring us sadness, stories that bring us joy but most importantly your spaces will open up the moments to be present and listen to one another's stories. Cherish that. You are making history and bringing so much for each generation you have before you.

References

Chapter 1

Beth Johnson Foundation. (2001). *Building better communities for all ages between the generations.* (Online). Available at: http://www.centreforip.org.uk

Blackstock, C. (2011). The emergence of the Breath of Life theory. *Journal of Social Work Values and Ethics*, 8(1). White Hat Communications.

Donne, J. ([1624]1988). No Man is an Island. London: Profile Books.

Linking Generations. (2021). *Care homes and intergenerational practice.* (Online). Available at: www.linkinggenerationsni.com/wp-content/uploads/2021/07/ACE-Care-and-IP-.pdf

Maslow, A.H. (1943). A theory of human motivation. *Psychological Review*, 50 (4).

Mass Live. (2021). *Massachusetts "must pursue" intergenerational care in post-pandemic recovery, says Senate President Karen Spilka.* (Online). Available at: www.masslive.com/politics/2021/10/massachusetts-must-pursue-intergenerational-care-in-post-pandemic-recovery-says-senate-president-karen-spilka.html

Morita, K. and Kobayashi, M. (2013). Interactive programs with preschool children bring smiles and conversation to older adults: time-sampling study. *BMC Geriatrics*, 13. (Online). Available at: https://bmcgeriatr.biomedcentral.com/track/pdf/10.1186/1471-2318-13-111.pdf

Scharf, T. and De Jong Giervield, J. (2008). Loneliness in urban neighborhoods: an Anglo-Dutch comparison. *European Journal of Ageing*, 5(2). (Online). Available at: www.researchgate.net/publication/226914263_Loneliness_in_urban_neighborhoods_An_Anglo-Dutch_comparison

UFAA. (2019). *The next generation: how intergenerational interactions improves life chances of children and young people.* (Online). Available at: https://docs.wixstatic.com/ugd/98d289_b66eb9bbed7f4315a0920d34bf6a4896.pdf

Villanueva, E. (2018). *Decolonizing Wealth*. Berrett-Koehler Publishers.

Chapter 2

Age UK. (2018). As Christmas approaches, Age UK finds 1.7 million older people in England haven't met up with a friend in a month. (Online). Available at: www.ageuk.org.uk/latest-press/articles/2018/december/christmas-loneliness-statistics/

Centre for Ageing Better. (2021). *Respect and social inclusion.* (Online). Available at: ageing-better.org.uk/respect-and-social-inclusion-age-friendly-communities

Yorkston, K., Bourgeois, M. and Baylor, C. (2012). Communication and aging. *PMC*, 21(2), pp. 309–319. (Online). Available at: www.ncbi.nlm.nih.gov/pmc/articles/PMC3074568/

Chapter 3

AgeNI. (2019). *Launch of age-friendly network*. Belfast. (Online). Available at: www.ageni.org/news/launch-of-age-friendly-network#:~:text=Age%20Friendly%20Network%20NI%20aims,Age%20Friendly%20planning%20and%20practices

Department for Digital, Culture, Media and Sport (DDCMS). (2018). *A connected society. A strategy for tackling loneliness*. London: UK Government. (Online). Available at: https://assets.publishing.service.gov.uk/government/uploads/system/uploads/attachment_data/file/936725/6.4882_DCMS_Loneliness_Strategy_web_Update_V2.pdf

European Commission. (2018). *Fairness, inequality and inter-generational mobility*. Brussels: European Commission. (Online). Available at: https://europa.eu/eurobarometer/surveys/detail/2166

Fondazione Giacomo Brodolini and the European Centre for Social Welfare Policy and Research. (2021). *Study on intergenerational fairness*. Brussels: European Commission. (Online). Available at: www.euro.centre.org/downloads/detail/4108

Generations United and The Eisner Foundation. (2018). *All in together. Creating spaces where young and old thrive*. Generations United and The Eisner Foundation. (Online). Available at: www.gu.org/app/uploads/2018/06/SignatureReport-Eisner-All-In-Together.pdf

Generations Working Together. (2017). *Generations Working Together. A Motion in Scottish Parliament (full text)*. Generations Working Together. (Online). Available at: https://generationsworkingtogether.org/news/generations-working-together-motion-full-text-11-10-2017

Good News Network. (2021). *A grocery line where slower is better: supermarkets open "chat checkouts" to combat loneliness among elderly*. Good News Network. (Online). Available at: www.goodnewsnetwork.org/a-checkout-line-where-slower-is-better-supermarket-jumbo/

Holt-Lunstad, J., Smith, T.B., Baker, M., Harris, T. and Stephenson, D. (2015). *Loneliness and social isolation as risk factors for morality: a meta-analytic review*. Brigham: BYU Scholars Archive. (Online). Available at: https://scholarsarchive.byu.edu/cgi/viewcontent.cgi?article=3024&context=facpub

Jo Cox Commission on Loneliness. (2017). *Combatting loneliness one conversation at a time*. 1st edn. London: Jo Cox Commission on Loneliness, pp. 1–13. Available at: https://d3n8a8pro7vhmx.cloudfront.net/jcf/pages/164/attachments/original/1620919309/rb_dec17_jocox_commission_finalreport.pdf?1620919309 [accessed 6 September 2022].

Kaplan, M., Larkin, E. and Hatton-Yeo, A. (2008). Leadership in intergenerational practice: in search of the exclusive "P" factor – passion. *Journal of Leadership Education*, 7(3). (Online). Available at: https://journalofleadershiped.org/jole_articles/leadership-in-intergenerational-practice-in-search-of-the-elusive-p-factor-passion/

Quinn, E. (2020). *Loneliness in Northern Ireland: a call to action*. Belfast: The Action Group on Loneliness Policy. (Online). Available at: https://harrymcanulty.com.au/wp-content/uploads/2021/02/Loneliness-in-Northern-Ireland-A-Call-to-action.pdf

Welsh Government. (2020). *Loneliness and social isolation: connected communities.* Cardiff: Welsh Government. (Online). Available at: https://gov.wales/loneliness-and-social-isolation-connected-communities

World Health Organization. (2021). *Global report on ageism.* Switzerland: United Nations. (Online). Available at: www.un.org/development/desa/dspd/wp-content/uploads/sites/22/2021/03/9789240016866-eng.pdf

Zolyomi, E. (2019). *Peer review on "strategies for supporting social inclusion at older age".* Brussels: European Commission. (Online). Available at: https://ec.europa.eu/social/main.jsp?langId=en&catId=1024&furtherNews=yes&newsId=9418

Chapter 4

Age UK. (2019). *The number of older people with some unmet need for care now stands at 1.5 million.* (Online). Available at: www.ageuk.org.uk/latest-press/articles/2019/november/the-number-of-older-people-with-some-unmet-need-for-care-now-stands-at-1.5-million/

Femia, E., Zarit, S., Blair, C., Jarrott, S. and Bruno, K. (2008). Intergenerational preschool experiences and the young child: potential benefits to development. *Early Childhood Research Quarterly*, 23(2): 272–287. doi: 10.1016/j.ecresq.2007.05.001. (Online). Available at: www.researchgate.net/publication/222179524_Intergenerational_preschool_experiences_and_the_young_child_Potential_benefits_to_development

Fox, M.J. (2020). *No Time Like the Future.* London: Headlines.

Generations Working Together. (2014). *Intergenerational approaches to improving health and wellbeing.* London: Generations Working Together. (Online). Available at: https://generationsworkingtogether.org/downloads/536a04c11694b-GWT%20web%20FINAL.pdf

Griffiths Report. (1988). Community care: agenda for action. London: HMSO.

Jarrott, S.E., Schroeder, A. and Perkins, O. (2008). *Intergenerational shared sites: saving dollars while making sense.* Washington: Generations United. (Online). Available at: www.gu.org/app/uploads/2018/05/SharedSites-Report-SavingDollarsWhileMakingSense.pdf

Robinson, K. (2006). Do schools kill creativity? (Video) TED Conferences. Available at: https://www.ted.com/talks/sir_ken_robinson_do_schools_kill_creativity

Robson, D. (2022). The happiness revolution: how to boost the well-being of society. *New Scientist.* (Online). Available at: www.newscientist.com/article/mg25333703-200-the-happiness-revolution-how-to-boost-the-well-being-of-society/

Rocks, S., Boccarini, G., Charlesworth, A., Idriss, O., McConkey, R. and Rachet-Jacquet, L. (2021). *Health and social care funding to 2024/25.* London: The Health Foundation. (Online). Available at: www.health.org.uk/publications/reports/health-and-social-care-funding-to-2024-25

The Health Act. (1999). Available at: www.legislation.gov.uk/ukpga/1999/8/contents [accessed 6 September 2022].

The King's Fund. (2022). *New analysis shows "widespread decline" in adult social care.* Available at: www.kingsfund.org.uk/press/press-releases/new-analysis-shows-widespread-decline-adult-social-care [accessed 6 September 2022].

Chapter 6

Bowlby, R. (2007). Babies and toddlers in non-parental daycare can avoid stress and anxiety if they develop a lasting secondary attachment bond with one carer who is consistently accessible to them. *Attachment and Human Development*, 9(4), 307–319. (Online). Available at: https://doi.org/10.1080/14616730701711516

Economic and Social Research Institute (ESRI). (2021). *Quarterly Economic Commentary*, Spring 2021. Available at: www.esri.ie/system/files/publications/QEC2021SPR_0.pdf

Filippatou, D. and Kaldi, S. (2010). The effectiveness of project-based learning on pupils with learning difficulties regarding academic performance, group work and motivation. *International Journal of Special Education*, 25 (1), 17–26. (Online). Available at: https://files.eric.ed.gov/fulltext/EJ890562.pdf

Larmer, J., Mergendoller, J. and Boss, S. (2015). *Setting the standard for project-based learning*. Alexandria, VA: ASCD. (Online). Available at: www.researchgate.net/publication/318822669_Setting_the_Standard_for_Project_Based_Learning_A_Proven_Approach_to_Rigorous_Classroom_Instruction

Linking Generations. (2021). *Education and intergenerational practice*. (Online). Available at: www.linkinggenerationsni.com/wp-content/uploads/2021/07/ACE-Education-and-IP-.pdf

Park, A-La. (2015). The effects of intergenerational programmes on children and young people. *International Journal of School and Cognitive Psychology*, 2(1), 1–5. (Online). Available at: www.semanticscholar.org/paper/The-Effects-of-Intergenerational-Programmes-on-and-Park/6522e11517ceb6af2a03dc8f2352240ec9d233ad

Roantree, B., Maitre, B., McTague, A. and Privalko, I. (2021). Intergenerational inequality. *Poverty, Income and Living Standards in Ireland*. Ireland: pp. 29–37. (Online). Available at: https://doi.org/10.26504/bkmnext412_chapter4

Robinson, K. (2007). Do schools kill creativity? (Video) TED Conferences. Available at: www.ted.com/talks/sir_ken_robinson_do_schools_kill_creativity

Chapter 7

Bradley, J. (2020). Four in five grandparents "usually" provide childcare. *The Scotsman*. Available at: www.scotsman.com/news/people/four-five-grandparents-usually-provide-childcare-2506005

Centre for Ageing Better. (2021). *Digital inclusion*. (Online). Available at: https://ageing-better.org.uk/digital-inclusion

Commission for Rural Communities. (2012). *Social isolation experienced by older people in rural communities*. Gloucester: Commission for Rural Communities, p. 16. (Online). Available at: www.basw.co.uk/system/files/resources/basw_111815-1_0.pdf [accessed 6 September 2022].

Holt-Lunstad, J., Smith, T.B., Baker, M., Harris, T. and Stephenson, D. (2015). Loneliness and social isolation as risk factors for mortality: a meta-analytic review. *Perspectives on Psychological Science*. March; 10(2): 227–237. (Online). doi: 10.1177/1745691614568352. PMID: 25910392. Available at: https://pubmed.ncbi.nlm.nih.gov/25910392/

McAlister, F. and Burgess, A. (2012). *Fatherhood: parenting programmes and policy.* Brazil: Fathers Institute. (Online). Available at: www.fatherhoodinstitute.org/wp-content/uploads/2012/07/Parenting-Programmes-and-Policy-Critical-Review-Full-Report.pdf

Men's Shed. (2021). *About Men's Shed.* Available at: https://menssheds.org.uk/

NHS. (2020). *About dementia.* Available at: www.nhs.uk/conditions/dementia/about/

Welsh Government. (2015). *Well-being of Future Generations (Wales) Act.* Cardiff: Welsh Government. (Online). Available at: www.legislation.gov.uk/anaw/2015/2/contents/enacted

World Health Organization. (2021). *Global report on ageism.* Switzerland: United Nations. (Online). Available at: www.un.org/development/desa/dspd/wp-content/uploads/sites/22/2021/03/9789240016866-eng.pdf

Chapter 8

Rickard, A. and Walsh, T. (2019). Policy, practice and process in team teaching: a pilot project with co-operating teachers and student teachers on school placement. *Irish Educational Studies*, 38(3): 309–326. (Online). doi: 10.1080/03323315.2019.1625798. Available at: www.tandfonline.com/doi/full/10.1080/03323315.2019.1625798

Chapter 9

Legislation.gov.uk. (2017). *Children Act 1989.* (Online). Available at: www.legislation.gov.uk/ukpga/1989/41/section/17

Syed, M. (2022). *Rebel Ideas.* London, England. John Murray Press.

Chapter 10

Eden Project Communities. (2017). *Social Eating Helps Connect Communities.* Eden Project Communities. (Online). Available at: www.edenprojectcommunities.com/blog/social-eating-helps-connect-communities

Chapter 13

Moshakis, A. (2019). Evolution of man: the rise and rise of the male wellness sector. *The Guardian.* (Online). Available at: www.theguardian.com/fashion/2019/mar/17/evolution-of-man-the-rise-and-rise-of-the-male-wellness-sector

Statista. (2022). *Size of the global anti-aging market 2020–2026.* America. (Online). Available at: www.statista.com/statistics/509679/value-of-the-global-anti-aging-market/

World Health Organization. (2021). *Global report on ageism.* Switzerland: United Nations. (Online). Available at: www.un.org/development/desa/dspd/wp-content/uploads/sites/22/2021/03/9789240016866-eng.pdf

Index

Note: Tables are indicated by **bold**.

Adjaye, David 36
age friendly network 26
age UK 8, 22, 33
ageism 24, 63, 64, 116, 117
Allen, Lesley 98–101
Alzheimer's 46
Apples & Honey, care home 8
Arden, Jacinda 34
Armagh, Co. 94
Arviso, Dana 12
Association of Colleges 25, 57
Attenborough, David 115–16

Baker, M. 27, 64
barriers 2, 3, 15, 20, 27, 30, 31, 39, 41, 48, 50–2, 58, 64, 67, **90**, 98, 104, 105, 112
Baylor, C. 16
Beacon Award, Association of Colleges 25, 57
Bennett, Lynne 66–7
Beth Johnson Foundation 5, 43, 80
Bhutan 33–5
'Big Lunch Campaign' (2017) 89
Blackfoot 7, 55, 65, 114
Blackstock, Cindy 7; Emergence of the Breath of Life Theory (2011) 7
Blair, C. 32
Boss, S. 53
Bourgeois, M. 16
Bowlby, John 56
Bowlby, Richard 56; attachments, secondary 56, 57
'Bring Me Sunshine' Club 100
budget 32, 60, 65, 75, 77, 89, **90**
buildings, educational 39, 42
Brownlee, Estelle 96
Bruno, K. 32

Canada 7
Care Home Friends 81
care needs 6, 32, 45
'Caring for People', 1989, White Paper 32
Catford 98
Centre for Ageing Better (2021) 15, 65
'Chat checkout' 28
'Chatty Benches' 37–8
Cheyenne River Territory 12
Child protection 85
climate change 75
'Closing the Gap' Report 59
co-location 8
Confucius 62
consent 93, 106
Corr, Kierna 70–1, 96–8
costs 29, 32, 33, 37, 41, 42, 59, 60, 64, 75, 82, 94, 98, 117
Cosy Club 94–6
County Tyrone 74, 101
Covid 1, 19, 29, 32, 34, 51, 58, 59
curriculum planning 73, 74

death 47, 48, 64
'Decade of Healthy Aging' plan, 2020 63
Decolonising Wealth (2018) 12
De Jong Gierveld, J. 13
dementia 8, 17, 46, 63, 100
Department for Communities (Northern Ireland) 26–7
Department for Digital, Culture, Media & Sport (DDCMS) 25
Deptford 119
Diamond Club 100–1
Diana, Princess of Wales 119
dietary needs 42, 76

Dilnot Commission 32
disabilities, learning 18, 53
discrimination 24, 62, 64, 116
diversity 1, 2, 10, 11, 25, 35, 57, 70, 80, 83, 84, 87, 100, 115
Duke of Edinburgh Award Scheme 100

early years 30, 46, 52–4, 56, 57, 59, 61, 65, 72, 76, 77, 92, 96, 102
Economic & Social Research Institute 59
Eisner Foundation 30
English & Literacy Modules 61
English as a Second Language (ESOL) 70
Europe 24, 27, 79, 118
European Centre for Social Welfare Policy & Research 24
European Commission 24
evaluations 7, 25, 26, 34, 40, 42, 47, 48, 52, 76, 77, 81, 89, **90**, 92, 94, 95, 98, 105–17
exercise 73, 77, 100

Femia, E. 32
Fermanagh, Co 21, 75
festivals 14; Christmas 22–3, **73**, 94–6, 100; Easter **73**; Harvest Festival 14–15; Valentine's **73**
Filippatou, D. 53
Finland/Finnish 33
First Nations 7
Fondazione Giacomo Brodolini 24
food & drink 14, 15, 19, 21, 28, 43, 68, 75, 76, 89, 95, 96, 120
Fox, M. J. 34
France/French 24, 29

generations, seven 7
generations united 30
generations working together 25–6, 34, 80
Gervin, Leah 58–9
Gibb, Nick 25
Good News Network 28
Grahame, Christine, MSP 25–6
grants 32, 80, 81
Greece 53
grief 48, 120
Griffiths 32

Harris, T. 27, 64
Hatton-Yeo, A. 30
Health Act, 1999 (UK) 32
health: emotional 5, 16, 33, 34, 47, 54, 55, 68, 70; mental 54, 64, 69, 97; physical 55, 63, 64
Health, Public 9, 27

Health & Safety 44, 85, 91
Health & Social Care 31, 32, 43, 60, 76, 88, 94
Health Foundation 32
hearing 17, 19
Holt-Lunstad, J. 27, 64
horticulture 77
hospitality 76
housing, social 36

ICT 21, 51, 75, 113
impairments, sensory 50, 63, 86
inspectors/inspections 44, 52, 95
Ireland 40, 59, 76
isolation, social 8, 13, 19, 24–9, 33, 38, 43, 54, 58, 62–4, **111**, 115, 117; *see also* loneliness
#IWill Movement 25

James, Jesse 99
Japan 8, 27
Jarrott, S. 32
Jo Cox Loneliness Commission 25
Johnston, Leah 54

Kaldi, S. 53
Kaplan, M. 30
Khan, Sadiq 36
Kline, Nancy 112; Thinking Round 112
Kindness Postbox 12, 19–22
King's Fund 32
Kobayashi, M. 8
Korea, South 79

Larkin, E. 30
Larmer, J. 53
Lewisham, Mayor of 101
life expectancy 33, 65
linking generations 8, 19, 22, 35, 40–1, 43, 51, 54, 60, 64, 66, 79–82
literacy skills 21, 61, 74, 75, 77, 86, 102
London 36, 98, 101, 116, 119
London School of Economics 34
loneliness 8, 12, 13, 22, 24–9, 56, 62, 63, 83, 101; *see also* isolation, social
Loneliness in Northern Ireland: A Call to Action (2020) 26

Madrid 37, 52
maintenance teams 42, 49
Manhattan 36
Martella, Frank 33
Masaharu, Shimada 8
Maslow, Abraham 7, 55; hierarchy of need 7

Massachusetts 9
Mayor of London 36
McAdam, Shirley-Anne 101–3
McCully Russell, Sarah 41, 60, 117
Men's Shed 19, 43
Mergendoller, J. 53
Minister for Older People and Independent Living (France) 29
Minister of State for Health (Singapore) 27
Minister of State for School Standards (UK): 25
Ministry of Health (Netherlands) 28
MONALISA Programme (France) 29
Montessori, Maria 65
Morita, K. 8
Moshakis, Alex 116
mortality risk 64

National Assistance Act, 1948 (UK) 31
National Health Service (UK)/NHS 63
needs, physical 87
Netherlands 28
New Labour 32
New York 36
New Zealand 34
Next Generation Report (2018) 10
Northern Ireland 26–7, 35, 40, 64, 72–3, 75, 79–81, 98

Older Americans' Act 30
'One Against Loneliness' Campaign 28
Open University 11
O'Toole, Nuala 12, 19–21
Oxford, University of 89

parenting 55, 56, 69
Park, A-La 55
Parkinson's 34
Peatlands Playgroup 72, 94
permission 20, 46, **89**, 106; letters 45, **93**
Pike, Rachel 54
planning, community 81, 115
playgrounds 27, 31, 37, 100
policy makers 9, 29, 30, 33, 38, 41, 45, 63, 64, 117
Portugal 71
pots of kindness 67
poverty 12, 36, 51; digital 65
Public Health Agency (Northern Ireland) 27

ratio levels 43
'Read on, Get on' strategy (2016) 74

reading buddies 74
reflection 38, 39, 46, 51, 68, 102, 117
Rickard, A. 76
risk assessments 44, 49, 84, **85**, 95
risk factors 44, 64
River Valley 7
Robinson, Ken (Sir) 34–5
role models 5, 11, 57, 62, 78
routine 11, 13, 39, 42, 55, 68, 71, 86, 106

safeguarding 44, 52
Sainsbury's, supermarket 89
Saskatchewan 7
Scharf, T. 13
Scotland, Scottish 26–7
Scotsman, The 69
Scottish Government 26
Scout Association 66
Singapore 27
Smith, Elaine 26
Smith, T. B. 27, 64
Snapmiam 29
social media 1, 2, 20, 46, 61, 65, 81, 86, 93, 116
Spain 37, 52
Spilka, Karen 9
stakeholders 40, 63, 80, 104
Statista 116
STEM 102
Stephenson, D. 27, 64
storytelling 2, 36, 61, **73**, 87, 118
Sugar Hill 36
sustainability 15, 16, 21, 22, 28, 36, 39–41, 52, 63, 67, 79, 82, 86, 92, 96, 101, 102, 105, 113
Sweden **73**, 98

technology 1, 16, 19, 29, 46, 50, 51, 60, 65–7, 75, 81, 86, 93, 100–2, 113, 118
TED Talks 34
timings 42, 85, **111**
Titterington, Vicki 22, 64, 79–82
toileting 49
Tokyo 8, 27
transport 42, 64, 69

UFAA 8, 10
UK Government 25
Ulster Museum 81
United Kingdom (UK) 8, 10, 12, 16, 24–7, 29, 31, 32, 37, 38, 40, 52, 57, 60, 63, 69, 89
United States of America 33, 36, 54

values 1, 5, 14, 20, 21, 30, 38, 46, 50, 57, 59, 76, *87*, 105, 115, 117, 118
Villanueva, Edgar 12
volunteers 11, 20, 26, 28, 44, 65, 74, 80, 81

Wales/Welsh 26–7, 63
Walsh, T. 76
War Memorial Organisation 81
Welfare State 31
'Well-being of Future Generations' Act, (2015): Wales 63
Welsh Government 26, 63

'White Cliffs of Dover' 99
Windmill Nursery 96–9
women in the workforce 9
Women's Institute 43
World Health Organization (WHO) 3, 5, 24, 63, 64, 117

Yvelines Student Programme 29
Yorkston, K. 16

Zarit, S. 32
Zolyomi, E. 28

For Product Safety Concerns and Information please contact our EU
representative GPSR@taylorandfrancis.com
Taylor & Francis Verlag GmbH, Kaufingerstraße 24, 80331 München, Germany

www.ingramcontent.com/pod-product-compliance
Lightning Source LLC
Chambersburg PA
CBHW071412300426
44114CB00016B/2279